D0826157

PULSE IT UP!

YOUR GUIDE TO UNLOCK THE POWER OF FOOD

150+ DELICIOUS RECIPES

Pascoe Publishing, Inc.
Rocklin, California

© 2011, Euro-Pro, LLC.

All rights reserved. No portion of this book may be reproduced by any means whatsoever without written permission from EuroPro, LLC., except for the inclusion of quotations in a media review.

Although every precaution has been taken in the preparation of this book, the publisher and authors assume no responsibility for errors or omissions. Nor is any liability assumed for damages resulting from the use of the information contained herein. Although every effort has been made to ensure that the information contained in this book is complete and accurate, neither the publisher nor the authors are engaged in rendering professional advice or services to the individual reader. This information is not intended to replace the advice of a medical practitioner and consumers should always consult with a health care professional prior to making changes to diet or lifestyle, including any new health-related eating programs. Neither the publisher nor author shall be held responsible for any loss or damage allegedly arising from any information or suggestion in this book. The opinions expressed in this book represent the personal views of the authors and not that of the publisher.

Nutritional Analyses: Calculations for the nutritional analyses in this book are based on the largest number of servings listed within the recipes. Calculations are rounded up to the nearest gram or milligram, as appropriate. If two options for an ingredient are listed, the first one is used. Not included are optional ingredients or serving suggestions.

Cover & Interior Design: KB Designs | Photography: Austin Blanco | Food Stylist: Michael Gadwa | Editor: Debi Bock

Published in the United States of America by

Pascoe Publishing, Inc.
Rocklin, California
www. pascoepublishing. com

ISBN: 978-1-929862-88-7

10 9 8 7 6 5 4 3 2 1

Printed in China

TABLE OF CONTENTS

CHAPTER 1 :: INTRODUCTION & HEALTH HIGHLIGHTS – P. 5

CHAPTER 2 :: APPETIZERS, SNACKS & SALSAS – P. 21

CHAPTER 3 :: COCKTAILS & PARTY DRINKS – P. 52

CHAPTER 4 :: SMOOTHIES & JUICES – P. 76

CHAPTER 5 :: SOUPS & SALADS – P. 112

CHAPTER 6 :: ENTRÉES & SIDE DISHES – P. 148

CHAPTER 7 :: BREADS & BAKERY GOODS – P. 176

CHAPTER 8 :: DELECTABLE DESSERTS – P. 202

SEASONAL FRUIT & VEGETABLE GUIDES – P. 223

EQUIVALENTS CHART – P. 224

NINJA

INTRODUCTION

Inside these pages, we've compiled the latest nutritional information to teach you how to combine ingredients to get the maximum healthful benefits from delicious and flavorful recipes. We aren't preaching to you to become a crazy health nut; we are simply offering a practical way to improve the things you blend, enabling a healthy lifestyle.

Although our goal in *Pulse it Up!* was to develop "healthy" recipes, our most important requirement was for each recipe to taste great! We know you don't have time to study this chapter, so we've made it easy for you to quickly identify the primary benefits of each recipe with our "Health Highlights". Each recipe outlines the main benefits on the side tabs of the page, allowing you to quickly choose recipes with the benefits you need. Whether you woke up feeling groggy and need a boost of energy to your morning, or you're looking for a dose of relaxation after a long day, you can quickly find delicious recipes tailored just for you!

The next few pages are your guide to understanding the Health Highlights and the Food Glossary that follows showcases some of nature's very best foods. So, go on…plug in your Ninja™ Kitchen System Pulse and blend delicious smoothies, knead dough into mouth-watering flatbreads and pastries, juice whole fruits and vegetables, and chop fresh ingredients for tasty snacks.

Above all… unlock the power of food and let our complete system inspire and simplify healthy living for your active on-the-go lifestyle.

Here's to your good health!

The Ninja™ Team

HEALTH HIGHLIGHTS

- ANTI-INFLAMMATORY
- IMMUNE BOOST
- MENTAL BOOST
- RELAXATION & STRESS RELIEF
- ANTI-AGING: SKIN, HAIR & EYE HEALTH
- DETOXIFY & MANAGE WEIGHT
- DIGESTION
- ENERGY BOOST

Inflammation is usually associated with swelling, redness and pain, but it's also your body's first response to infection. It is linked to poor eating habits and obesity. If eaten on a regular basis, anti-inflammatory foods help bring a balance to inflammation in your body.

anti-inflammatory

"Antioxidants" seems to be a buzz word these days, but what's the real benefit? First, antioxidants fight off the over-production of free radicals. Second, these super-nutrients promote good health by fighting infections and diseases. And, in addition, they provide energy and even support skin health!

immune boost

Some days you feel like you're ready to take on the world… other days you feel like you're in a fog, un-motivated, and you find it hard to focus. When you're having one of "those" days, enjoy brain-boosting foods to help you feel more alert and focused.

mental boost

A bit of relaxation can go a long way and these foods help your body to naturally relax. These foods might not help you meet a deadline or pay off your mortgage any faster, but they will help you feel more calm and cool. Eat your way to a less stressful life!

relaxation & stress relief

We all want truly fabulous skin, but who wants to pay hundreds of dollars for the latest skin cream, hair treatment, or spa day? Certain foods can help your skin look more radiant, your hair shinier, and do we dare say… help you look younger?!

anti-aging: skin, hair & eye health

These foods will help your body naturally filter, cleanse, and extract nutrients efficiently. Certain foods have natural cleansing properties that help rid your body of the extra junk you put in and can help naturally curb your appetite!

detoxify & manage weight

Many digestive-related problems are directly associated with what you eat. These foods can help naturally balance your digestive system, provide digestive-related aid, and are high in nutritional value.

digestion

Have you ever been so tired at work that you fall asleep at your desk? Or even worse, nod off in a meeting? Keep these foods stashed at your desk to help fill you up, provide natural energy, and stay alert.

energy boost

SUPER FOODS
ANTI-INFLAMMATORY

VEGETABLES	FRUITS	NUTS & SEEDS	HERBS & SPICES	OTHER
Tomatoes	Apples	Almonds	Basil	Cod
Avocados	Blueberries	Flaxseed/Linseed	Cayenne/Chili Peppers	Halibut
Bell Peppers	Fresh Pineapple	Hazelnuts	Cinnamon/Cloves	Oysters
Bok Choy	Guavas	Sunflower Seeds	Cocoa (70%+ cocoa)	Salmon
Broccoli	Kiwi	Walnuts	Licorice	Shrimp
Brussels Sprouts	Lemons/ Limes		Mint	Tuna
Cabbage	Oranges		Oregano	Turkey
Cauliflower	Papaya		Parsley	Lamb
Chard	Raspberries		Rosemary	
Fennel	Strawberries		Thyme	
Bulb Garlic	Pineapple		Turmeric	
Green Beans				
Green/Spring Onions				
Kale				
Leeks				
Olives				
Spinach				
Sweet Potatoes				
Turnip Greens				

SUPER FOODS
IMMUNE BOOST

VEGETABLES	FRUITS	NUTS & SEEDS	HERBS & SPICES	OTHER
Garlic	Blueberries	Pecans	Turmeric	Yogurt
Mushrooms	Lemons	Almonds	Black Pepper	Pinto Beans
Sweet Potatoes	Grapefruit	Flaxseed	Oregano	Kidney Beans
Carrots	Tangerines		Cinnamon	Black Beans
Cucumbers	Oranges		Cloves	
Pumpkin	Grapes		Ginger	
Squash	Raisins		Cayenne Pepper	
Cabbage	Plums		Sage	
Spinach	Strawberries		Thyme	
Kale	Raspberries		Basil	
Peppers	Cherries			
Brussels Sprouts	Watermelon			
Broccoli	Nectarines			
Peppers	Peaches			
Artichokes	Mangos			
Russet Potatoes	Melon			
Green Beans	Apricots			
Tomato	Blackberries			
	Apples			
	Cranberries			
	Pineapple			
	Kiwi			

SUPER FOODS
MENTAL BOOST

VEGETABLES	FRUITS	NUTS & SEEDS	HERBS & SPICES	OTHER
Beets	Blueberries	Walnuts	Turmeric	Salmon
Broccoli	Lemons/Limes	Cashews	Rosemary	Eggs
Carrots	Oranges	Peanuts		Coffee, Freshly Ground
Romaine Lettuce	Grapefruit	Flaxseed		Beans
Spinach	Apricots			Kidney Beans
Swiss Chard	Mangos			Pinto Beans
Arugula	Cantaloupe			Shrimp
Kale	Watermelon			
Tomatoes	Strawberries			
Radishes	Blackberries			
Eggplant	Raspberries			
	Cranberries			
	Cherries			
	Plums			

SUPER FOODS
RELAXATION & STRESS RELIEF

VEGETABLES	FRUITS	NUTS & SEEDS	HERBS & SPICES	OTHER
Broccoli	Blueberries	Walnuts	Basil	Low fat/Skim Milk
Kale	Oranges	Almonds	Arugula	Brown Rice
Brussels Sprouts	Bananas	Pistachios		Salmon
Asparagus	Apples	Pumpkin Seeds		Shrimp
Cabbage	Pomegranates	Sunflower Seeds		Scallops
Artichokes	Pineapple			Tuna
Sweet Potatoes	Apricots			
Avocados	Papayas			
Black Beans				
Corn				
White Beans				
Potatoes				
Lentils				
Chickpeas				
Spinach				
Swiss Chard				
Asparagus				

SUPER FOODS
ANTI-AGING: SKIN, HAIR & EYE HEALTH

VEGETABLES	FRUITS	NUTS & SEEDS	HERBS & SPICES	OTHER
Avocado	Watermelon	Pumpkin Seeds	Ginger	Herring
Garlic	Blackberries	Sunflower Seeds	Cinnamon	Salmon
Broccoli	Blueberries	Walnuts	Sage	Shrimp
Cherry Tomatoes	Strawberries	Brazil Nuts		Fresh Tuna
Spinach	Red Grapes	Almonds		Dark Chocolate
Red Onions	Cranberries			Kidney Beans
Cauliflower	Raspberries			Pinto Beans
Cucumbers	Oranges			Yogurt
Kale	Cherries			Cottage Cheese
Turnips	Plums			
Brussels Sprouts	Mangos			
Cabbage	Grapefruit			
Radish	Peaches			
Artichoke Hearts	Cantaloupe			
Carrots	Pineapple			
Squash	Kiwi			
Bok Choy	Honeydew			
Peas				

SUPER FOODS
DETOXIFY & MANAGE WEIGHT

VEGETABLES	FRUITS	NUTS & SEEDS	HERBS & SPICES	OTHER
Artichoke	Blackberries	Flaxseed	Cayenne Pepper	Salmon
Broccoli	Blueberries	Sunflower Seeds	Ginger	Eggs
Cauliflower	Cherries	Pine Nuts	Cinnamon	Shrimp
Green Beans	Purple Grapes		Horseradish	Lean Meats
Sweet Potatoes	Kiwi		Red Chili Peppers	Yogurt
Yams	Papayas			Milk
Beans	Prunes			Cheese
Spinach	Raspberries			
Asparagus	Strawberries			
Tomatoes	Grapefruit			
Mushrooms	Apples			
Cucumbers	Watermelon			
Peppers	Cantaloupe			
Celery				
Carrots				

SUPER FOODS
DIGESTION

VEGETABLES	FRUITS	NUTS & SEEDS	HERBS & SPICES	OTHER
Garlic	Apples	Sunflower Seeds	Mint	Yogurt
Avocados	Bananas	Flaxseed Oil	Cumin	Rice
Cabbage	Blackberries	Almonds	Fennel	Tofu
Onion	Blueberries		Oregano	Eggs
Squash	Cherries		Curry Powder	
Cucumbers	Purple Grapes		Paprika	
Broccoli	Papaya		Basil	
Romaine Lettuce	Lemons		Sage	
Kale	Raisins		Cumin	
Onions	Mangos		Mustard	
Beans			Garlic	
			Cinnamon	
			Paprika	
			Coriander	
			Cayenne Pepper	
			Ginger	
			Clove	
			Coriander	

SUPER FOODS
ENERGY BOOST

VEGETABLES	FRUITS	NUTS & SEEDS	HERBS & SPICES	OTHER
Beans	Oranges	Almonds	Parsley	Yogurt
Spinach	Watermelon	Pumpkin Seeds	Cilantro	Eggs
Romaine Lettuce	Blackberries	Hazelnuts		Salmon
Corn	Blueberries	Cashews		Lean Meats
Sweet Potatoes	Raspberries	Flaxseeds		Tuna
Spinach	Apples			Shrimp
Celery	Strawberries			Whole Grain Pasta
Cucumbers	Kiwi			Dark Chocolate
Mushrooms	Cantaloupe			Steak
Lentils	Bananas			
Avocados	Grapefruit			
Watercress	Pears			
Arugula	Lemons			
Kale				
Beans				

APPLES

THE ADVANTAGE:

- Really strong antioxidant power!
- A true healing-power food
- The second-highest level of antioxidant activity of any consumed fruit
- Valuable source of fiber, which can lower cholesterol
- Contains the highest source of Boron, a mineral that assists in bone-building.

FOOD FOR THOUGHT:

- The apple peel has the most potent antioxidant activity.
- Purchased apple juice may have added sugar and preservatives, along with higher calories. Make your own at home as the best alternative.

anti-inflammatory
immune boost
relaxation & stress relief
detoxify & manage weight
digestion
energy boost

BANANAS

THE ADVANTAGE:

- Bananas are a rich source of Vitamin B6, which may prolong mental health, according to the USDA.
- High in potassium and fiber

FOOD FOR THOUGHT:

- Bananas are rich in potassium, which can help maintain body fluids, assist heart health, balance electrolytes, reduce muscle cramps, and elevate energy levels.
- Assists in good digestive health.
- The inner peel is one of the most nutritional parts! Scrape the inner peel into your smoothie for an added nutritional boost!

relaxation & stress relief
digestion
energy boost

BLUEBERRIES

THE ADVANTAGE:

- This little fruit packs a big punch that helps keep your memory sharp and your brain stimulated.
- One of the most powerful fruits to include in your diet
- Blueberries provide strong antioxidant power, act as an anti-inflammatory, and may help with your memory.

FOOD FOR THOUGHT:

- Either fresh or frozen berries deliver the same delicious, healthy benefits.
- Blue and Purple fruit are memory-boosters.

anti-inflammatory
immune boost
mental boost
relaxation & stress relief
anti-aging
detoxify & manage weight
digestion
energy boost

CANTALOUPE

The Advantage:

- Cantaloupe is your best friend in weight control. Why? It is a high-volume fruit that curbs hunger: high in fiber, water and air, yet low in calories. Your body thinks you're full faster, with less craving for more.
- Rich in potassium and Vitamin A, which helps heart-health, blood pressure, vision, growth and bone-building.
- High in Vitamin C!
- One of the best immune boosters among all fruits!

FOOD FOR THOUGHT:

- Cantaloupe is rich in Vitamin A as a beta carotene. It helps protect against cell damage and is a great antioxidant.

TASTE THE ADVANTAGE:

- Mix cantaloupe with watermelon, club soda, and fresh ginger for a refreshing treat.

mental boost
anti-aging
detoxify & manage weight
energy boost

RASPBERRIES

THE ADVANTAGE:

- A fiber powerhouse!
- The benefits don't stop there; raspberries have magnesium and, not to mention, are low in calories.
- Help replace dying cells with healthy cells, may help with inflammation and pain.
- Significant antioxidant boost.

FOOD FOR THOUGHT:

- This fruit is fragile: we recommend buying fresh and organic for best nutritional value and flavor satisfaction.
- Highest count of fiber among the most commonly eaten berries.

anti-inflammatory
immune boost
mental boost
anti-aging
detoxify & manage weight
energy boost

STRAWBERRIES

THE ADVANTAGE:

- Potent antioxidant berry.
- Offers the most Vitamin C of any other commonly consumed berry.
- Red fruits can help improve blood flow and are thought to help prevent Alzheimer's disease.

FOOD FOR THOUGHT:

- 1 cup of strawberries equals about 50 calories and offers around 3g of fiber and around 85mg of Vitamin C.
- Noted as one of the most contaminated fruits. Buy organic to get the best flavor and quality.
- Frozen strawberries offer the same health benefits as fresh, a great alternative year round.
- High in disease-fighting phytochemicals.

anti-inflammatory
immune boost
mental boost
anti-aging
detoxify & manage weight
energy boost

PINEAPPLE

THE ADVANTAGE:

- Powerful anti-inflammatory powers.
- Contains Bromelain enzymes, natural blood thinners, that can aid in digestion, healing and inflammation.
- Provides fiber, Vitamin C, potassium, and other minerals for general good health.
- Yellow and Orange fruits help prevent eye disease and act as an immune boost.

FOOD FOR THOUGHT:

- One of the most powerful natural digestive reliefs.
- 1 cup of fresh pineapple has almost 100% of the daily value for manganese. Manganese is essential for healthy skin, cartilage formation and bones.

anti-inflammatory
immune boost
relaxation & stress relief
anti-aging

ORANGES

THE ADVANTAGE:

- A massive boost of Vitamin C, a premier antioxidant.
- Provides support for better heart and digestive health and lowers the risk of infections, inflammation and stroke.
- May also improve healthful cholesterol.
- Contains high amounts of calcium, which promotes strong bones and teeth.

FOOD FOR THOUGHT:

- Studies have shown citrus fruits may lower the risk of some cancers.
- Pulp is your friend! Pulp contains the healthiest nutrients in fruits, providing many vitamin compounds, minerals and fiber.

anti-inflammatory
immune boost
mental boost
relaxation & stress relief
anti-aging
energy boost

KIWI

THE ADVANTAGE:

- A super-fruit, rich with antioxidants, that can help in healing.
- Kiwis have the highest level of Vitamin C, twice that of oranges.
- A good source of Vitamin E, potassium, and fiber.

FOOD FOR THOUGHT:

- Kiwi works as a natural blood thinner.
- Green fruits can help protect bones and teeth, and aid in eyesight.
- A natural meat tenderizer, cut kiwi in half and rub on meat before cooking.

anti-inflammatory
immune boost
anti-aging
detoxify & manage weight
energy boost

WATERMELON

THE ADVANTAGE:

- One of the healthiest foods! Watermelon helps curb your appetite and provides high levels of lycopene and Vitamin A.
- A high-volume food which aids in managing weight.
- Great source of vitamin A as a beta-carotene that helps fight free radicals, essential for eye and immune health.

FOOD FOR THOUGHT:

- Helps support eye and immune health via Vitamin A (in beta-carotene), which helps fight free radicals.
- Watermelon is great after a workout. It can help re-hydrate your body and restore electrolyte balance.

immune boost
mental boost
anti-aging
detoxify & manage weight
energy boost

AVOCADOS

THE ADVANTAGE:

- Although high in fat; the fact is, it's a healthy HDL fat. Monounsaturated fat is an omega-9 that may actually lower cholesterol.
- Contains lutein from the carotene family that acts as an antioxidant to aid in eye, heart and skin health.
- Avocados are a great source of fiber, potassium, folate, Vitamin A, Vitamin E, Zinc and beta-carotene.
- Rich in folate, in the Vitamin B family, that may help prevent birth defects.

FOOD FOR THOUGHT:

- Research studies link avocados to lower blood pressure and cholesterol counts. Helpful in maintaining bone and immune health.

anti-inflammatory
relaxation & stress relief
anti-aging
digestion

KALE

THE ADVANTAGE:

- Superstar vegetable! The #1 antioxidant food that fights cell-damaging free radicals.
- Contains phyto-chemicals that have been shown to have protective effects against many cancers.
- Loaded with calcium, Vitamin A, C, K, and iron.
- Terrific source of fiber and protein.

FOOD FOR THOUGHT:

- Kale has seven times the beta-carotene of broccoli.

anti-inflammatory
immune boost
mental boost
relaxation & stress relief
anti-aging

TOMATOES

THE ADVANTAGE:

- Provides extremely beneficial anti-cancer properties when consumed with fat-rich foods such as avocados. Fat-rich foods help the absorption of lycopene.
- Tomatoes contain multiple antioxidant agents that have strong disease fighting power.
- A mega dose of Vitamin C, rich in potassium and magnesium, this powerful combo is a great choice to restore your body after a workout.

FOOD FOR THOUGHT:

- May be especially good for men; the antioxidant compounds have been shown to fight prostate cancer.

immune boost
mental boost
anti-aging
detoxify & manage weight

SPINACH

THE ADVANTAGE:

- One of the best sources of Vitamin K, critical for building strong bones. Vitamin K works with calcium to make sure you get the minerals into your bones.
- It's also rich in Vitamin A, manganese, folic acid, magnesium, iron, and quercetin (anti-inflamatory compound).
- Promotes good health as an antioxidant and anti-cancer support.
- May help lower cholesterol and blood pressure while assisting eye and heart-health. Can also help reduce inflammation.

FOOD FOR THOUGHT:

- Spinach provides more nutrients than almost any other food.
- One of the lowest calorie foods on the planet.
- A great alternative to milk for Vitamin C.

anti-inflammatory
immune boost
mental boost
relaxation & stress relief
anti-aging
detoxify & manage weight
energy boost

BROCCOLI

THE ADVANTAGE:

- Strong antioxidant and aid in detoxifying.
- 1 cup of broccoli contains more than 40mg of calcium, 81 mg of Vitamin C, 2g of protein and fiber, a whopping 1,277 mcg of Vitamin A, plus folate, magnesium, phosphorus and beta-carotene.
- Great for bone, teeth, and eye health.

FOOD FOR THOUGHT:

- Broccoli has been shown to help fight cancers by neutralizing carcinogens that destroy cancerous cells.
- May be especially good for women; broccoli is linked to reducing the risk of breast and cervical cancer.

anti-inflammatory
immune boost
mental boost
relaxation & stress relief
anti-aging
detoxify & manage weight

CARROTS

THE ADVANTAGE:

- Contains a high level of carotenoids, which are associated with decreasing the risk of cancer.
- A great source of lutein, which provides eye health.
- Antioxidant and immune system stimulator, helpful in fighting infections.
- Rich source of calcium, potassium, Vitamin A and sprinkled with magnesium, phosphorus and fiber.
- Fantastic for detoxifying!

FOOD FOR THOUGHT:

- Recent studies have indicated a carrot a day could cut the rate of lung cancer.
- Yellow and Orange fruits help with eye health and can boost your immune system.

immune boost
mental boost
anti-aging
detoxify & manage weight

FIERY CHILE SHRIMP WITH FRESH ARUGULA – P. 26
QUICK & EASY GOLDEN TREASURE CARROTS – P. 27
BLACK BEAN DIP WITH MELTED GOAT CHEESE – P. 28
ITALIAN BRUSCHETTA WITH CREAMY BALSAMIC SPREAD – P. 29
FAST & FRESH SPINACH & CHEDDAR CHEESE QUICHE – P. 30
EDAMAME DIP WITH BROCCOLI FLORETS – P. 31
SMOKED SALMON SPREAD – P. 32
ZUCCHINI ROLLS STUFFED WITH HERBED GOAT CHEESE – P. 33
TOMATO BASIL BRUSCHETTA – P. 34
PINEAPPLE & RED ONION SALSA – P. 35
CHERRY TOMATO BITES – P. 36
EAST INDIAN SPICED LENTIL DIP WITH NAAN BREAD – P. 37

CHAPTER TWO :: APPETIZERS, SNACKS & SALSAS

FIRE-ROASTED TOMATO SALSA WITH TORTILLA CHIPS – P. 38
TOMATILLO SALSA VERDE – P. 39
THAI LETTUCE WRAPS WITH PEANUT DIPPING SAUCE – P. 40
DUXELLE CUCUMBER CUPS – P. 41
MELON CUCUMBER SALSA – P. 42
BACON & CHEDDAR STUFFED BOULE – P. 43
BLUE CHEESE & WALNUT STUFFED PORTABELLO MUSHROOMS – P. 44
CHILLED JUMBO SHRIMP WITH SWEET CHILI DIPPING SAUCE – P. 45
CRUDITES WITH COOL ARTICHOKE-SPINACH DIP – P. 46
SALSA GUACAMOLE – P. 47
GREEN GODDESS DIP WITH TENDER-CRISP GREEN BEANS – P. 48
JAPANESE PORK POTSTICKERS WITH SPICY ASIAN DIPPING SAUCE – P. 49
CRISP CAULIFLOWER WITH LEMON TAHINI SAUCE – P. 50
PARMESAN WHOLE WHEAT BREAD CRUMBS – P. 51

SPEEDY CHICKEN TORTILLA SOUP – P. 131

THREE BEAN SALAD WITH ITALIAN HERB VINAIGRETTE – P. 143

CORNISH BEEF PASTIES – P. 168

AVOCADO SHAKE – P. 88

FIERY CHILE SHRIMP WITH FRESH ARUGULA

1 TBSP. TOASTED SESAME OIL
2 TBSP. RICE WINE VINEGAR (OR 1 TBSP. WHITE VINEGAR)
2 TBSP. WATER
½ SMALL SERRANO PEPPER (OR TO TASTE), ROUGHLY CUT
½ SMALL TOMATO
½ SMALL WHITE ONION, ROUGHLY CUT
2 CLOVES GARLIC, PEELED
2 TBSP. FRESH CILANTRO LEAVES
SALT & PEPPER TO TASTE
20 LARGE COOKED SHRIMP, DEVEINED AND TAILS REMOVED
6 OZ. FRESH ARUGULA, WASHED AND DRAINED

Place all ingredients, except the shrimp and arugula, in the 40 oz. Processing Bowl and pulse until lightly chopped. Remove and place in a medium bowl. To serve, arrange the shrimp on arugula leaves on 4 small plates and spoon the fiery tomato topping over each. Serve immediately or chill until serving. Serves 4.

CAL 75, FAT 0G, SAT FAT 0G, CHOL 47MG, SODIUM 53MG,
CARBS 4G, PROTEIN 2G, FIBER 1G, CALCIUM 25MG, POTASSIUM 203MG

QUICK & EASY
GOLDEN TREASURE CARROTS

2 TBSP. ORANGE JUICE
8 OZ. LOW FAT CREAM CHEESE, AT ROOM TEMPERATURE
2 TBSP. RAW, UNFILTERED HONEY
⅛ TSP. GROUND GINGER
⅛ TSP. GROUND CINNAMON
1 LB. FRESH CARROTS, PEELED, CUT INTO ¼ INCH-THICK COINS, BLANCHED AND CHILLED (OR SERVE FRESH, RAW CARROT COINS, IF DESIRED)

Place the orange juice, cream cheese, honey, and spices in the 40 oz. Processing Bowl. Pulse until smooth. Spoon into a small bowl and serve with the chilled carrot coins. Serves 4 to 6.

CAL 144, FAT 7G, SAT FAT 4G, CHOL 21MG, SODIUM 164MG,
CARBS 16G, PROTEIN 5G, FIBER 2G, CALCIUM 69MG, POTASSIUM 326MG

BLACK BEAN DIP
WITH MELTED GOAT CHEESE

15 OZ. CAN BLACK BEANS, DRAINED, LIQUID RESERVED
1 CLOVE GARLIC, PEELED
1 TBSP. FRESH CILANTRO LEAVES
2 TSP. FRESH LIME JUICE
½ TSP. GROUND CUMIN
¼ TSP. CHILI POWDER (OR MORE, TO TASTE)
¼ TSP. SALT
4 OZ. GOAT CHEESE, CRUMBLED
FRESH VEGETABLES FOR DIPPING: BROCCOLI FLORETS, RED PEPPER STRIPS, CELERY, CAULIFLOWER FLORETS, ETC.

Preheat oven to 375°F. Place all ingredients, except the goat cheese, in the 40 oz. Processing Bowl. Pulse until smooth.

Place the bean dip in an oven-proof serving dish and top with the goat cheese. Bake for 10-12 minutes, or until the goat cheese has melted. Serve with fresh vegetables for dipping. Serves 6 to 8.

CAL 116, FAT 3G, SAT FAT 2G, CHOL 2MG, SODIUM 31MG, CARBS 14G, PROTEIN 5G, FIBER 5G, CALCIUM 20MG, POTASSIUM 243MG

ITALIAN BRUSCHETTA
WITH CREAMY BALSAMIC SPREAD

1 BAGUETTE, SLICED INTO ¼ INCH-THICK ROUNDS
¼ CUP EXTRA VIRGIN OLIVE OIL
6 OZ. CAN SLICED BLACK OLIVES, DIVIDED
14 OZ. CAN GARBANZO BEANS, DRAINED
1 TBSP. BALSAMIC VINEGAR
¼ TSP. RED PEPPER FLAKES
1 CLOVE GARLIC, PEELED
1 TSP. SALT
¼ TSP. GROUND BLACK PEPPER
2 TBSP. FLAT-LEAF PARSLEY, CHOPPED, FOR GARNISH

Preheat the broiler to High. Brush each baguette slice generously with olive oil on one side and place on the broiler pan, oiled side up. Broil until toasted and set aside.

Place one-half of the olives and the remaining ingredients, except the parsley, in the 40 oz. Processing Bowl. Pulse until smooth. To serve, spoon a small amount of the balsamic spread on each toast and garnish with the remaining sliced olives and parsley. Serves 6 to 8.

CAL 265, FAT 8G, SAT FAT 1G, CHOL 0MG, SODIUM 1064MG, CARBS 44G, PROTEIN 8G, FIBER 5G, CALCIUM 29MG, POTASSIUM 156MG

FAST & FRESH SPINACH & CHEDDAR CHEESE QUICHE

1 SHEET REFRIGERATED PIE DOUGH
6 LARGE EGGS
2 TBSP. LOW FAT MILK
1 CUP FRESH SPINACH LEAVES, ROUGHLY CUT
3 OZ. CHEDDAR CHEESE, SHREDDED
2 GREEN ONIONS, ROUGHLY CUT
1 TSP. SALT
¼ TSP. GROUND BLACK PEPPER

Unfold the pastry sheet into a large 14-inch sauté pan and cut the pastry in a circle to fit the bottom of the pan only. Cook the pastry crust on medium-low heat for 5 to 6 minutes, or until firm on the bottom. Using a wide spatula, flip the pastry and continue cooking for 3 to 4 minutes.

Place the remaining ingredients in the 40 oz. Processing Bowl and pulse until the spinach and onions are chopped. Pour the egg mixture over the pastry. Cover and cook over medium heat until the eggs are set and the quiche is cooked throughout, about 8 to 10 minutes. Slice into thin wedges and serve while warm. Serves 8.

CAL 200, FAT 13G, SAT FAT 6G, CHOL 152MG, SODIUM 543MG,
CARBS 13G, PROTEIN 8G, FIBER 0G, CALCIUM 77MG, POTASSIUM 90MG

EDAMAME DIP
WITH BROCCOLI FLORETS

16 OZ. PACKAGE FROZEN SHELLED EDAMAME, BLANCHED
2 TBSP. SOY SAUCE (OR USE LOW SODIUM SOY SAUCE)
½ CUP FRESH CILANTRO LEAVES
¼ CUP SWEET ONION, ROUGHLY CUT
1 CLOVE GARLIC, PEELED
2 TBSP. EXTRA VIRGIN OLIVE OIL
½ CUP SOUR CREAM (USE LOW FAT, IF PREFERRED)
2 MEDIUM HEADS BROCCOLI, CUT INTO FLORETS

Place all ingredients, except the broccoli, in the 40 oz. Processing Bowl. Pulse until very smooth. Spoon the edamame dip into a serving bowl and serve with the broccoli florets for dipping. Serves 6.

CAL 237, FAT 14G, SAT FAT 4G, CHOL 9MG, SODIUM 345MG,
CARBS 15G, PROTEIN 14G, FIBER 7G, CALCIUM 196MG, POTASSIUM 871MG

SMOKED SALMON SPREAD

8 OZ. LOW FAT CREAM CHEESE, AT ROOM TEMPERATURE.
¼ CUP LOW FAT SOUR CREAM
¼ CUP LOW FAT GREEK YOGURT
1 TBSP. FRESH LEMON JUICE
2 TSP. FRESH DILL, PLUS MORE FOR GARNISH
2 TSP. CHIVES (OR GREEN ONIONS), PLUS MORE FOR GARNISH
½ TSP. SALT
¼ TSP. GROUND BLACK PEPPER
4 OZ. SMOKED SALMON, ROUGHLY CHOPPED
THINLY SLICED RYE BREAD ROUNDS

Place the cream cheese, sour cream, yogurt, lemon juice, dill, chives, salt, pepper, and half of the smoked salmon in the 40 oz. Processing Bowl. Pulse until smooth.

Place the spread in a serving dish and mix in the remaining salmon by hand. Garnish with dill and chives, if desired. Serve right away with rye bread rounds or chill until serving. Serves 8.

CAL 95, FAT 6G, SAT FAT 4G, CHOL 20MG, SODIUM 347MG,
CARBS 3G, PROTEIN 7G, FIBER 0G, CALCIUM 54MG, POTASSIUM 74MG

ZUCCHINI ROLLS STUFFED WITH HERBED GOAT CHEESE

8 OZ. FRESH GOAT CHEESE, AT ROOM TEMPERATURE
2 TBSP. LOW FAT MILK
1 TBSP. FRESH MINT LEAVES
1 TBSP. FRESH BASIL LEAVES
1 TBSP. FRESH CHIVES
1 TSP. LEMON ZEST (OR JUICE, IF DESIRED)
3 LARGE ZUCCHINI, SLICED LENGTHWISE INTO ¼-INCH SLICES AND BROILED OR GRILLED

Place all of the ingredients, except the zucchini, in the 40 oz. Processing Bowl. Pulse until smooth.

Put one-half teaspoon of the cheese mixture about one-half inch from the end of each cooled zucchini slice. Roll up each slice and place seam side down on a serving platter. Secure with toothpicks, if needed. Serve right away or chill until serving. Serves 4 to 6.

CAL 166, FAT 9G, SAT FAT 6G, CHOL 23MG, SODIUM 160MG,
CARBS 5G, PROTEIN 2G, FIBER 1G, CALCIUM 29MG, POTASSIUM 368MG

TOMATO BASIL BRUSCHETTA

2 MEDIUM ROMA TOMATOES, SEEDED, CORED, AND QUARTERED
1 CLOVE GARLIC, PEELED
10 LARGE FRESH BASIL LEAVES
2 TBSP. EXTRA VIRGIN OLIVE OIL
1 TBSP. CAPERS
1 BAGUETTE, SLICED INTO ¼-INCH THICK ROUNDS, TOASTED

Place the tomatoes, garlic, basil and olive oil in the 40 oz. Processing Bowl. Pulse just until roughly chopped. Mix in the capers by hand.

Place a tablespoon of the tomato mixture on each baguette round and arrange the bruschetta on a serving platter. Serve right away. Serves 4 to 6.

CAL 195, FAT 6G, SAT FAT 1G, CHOL 0MG, SODIUM 414MG,
CARBS 31G, PROTEIN 0G, FIBER 1G, CALCIUM 9MG, POTASSIUM 54MG

PINEAPPLE & RED ONION SALSA

¼ CUP RED ONION, ROUGHLY CUT
3 TBSP. FRESH CILANTRO LEAVES
2 CUPS FRESH PINEAPPLE, ROUGHLY CUT
1 TBSP. RAW, UNFILTERED HONEY
2 TBSP. FRESH LIME JUICE

Place all the ingredients in the 40 oz. Processing Bowl and pulse quickly, just until chunky. Serve right away over mild white fish or poultry. Serves 6 to 8.

CAL 49, FAT 0G, SAT FAT 0G, CHOL 0MG, SODIUM 2MG,
CARBS 14G, PROTEIN 0G, FIBER 1G, CALCIUM 1MG, POTASSIUM 115MG

CHERRY TOMATO BITES

24 LARGE CHERRY TOMATOES
1 LARGE RIPE AVOCADO, SEEDED AND SKIN REMOVED
4 OZ. FETA CHEESE, CRUMBLED
1 TBSP. LEMON JUICE
3 TBSP. CHIVES
SALT TO TASTE

Slice ¼-inch off the bottom of each tomato, reserving the slices. Remove the juice, seeds, and flesh from the inside of each cherry tomato. Set aside, stem side down.

Place the remaining ingredients in the 40 oz. Processing Bowl. Pulse until smooth.

Place 1 teaspoon of the avocado mixture into each cherry tomato. Top each with a reserved tomato slice. Makes 24 appetizers.

CAL 124, FAT 9G, SAT FAT 4G, CHOL 17MG, SODIUM 239MG,
CARBS 8G, PROTEIN 3G, FIBER 2G, CALCIUM 10MG, POTASSIUM 177MG

EAST INDIAN SPICED LENTIL DIP WITH NAAN BREAD

1 TBSP. FRESH LEMON JUICE
1 TBSP. EXTRA VIRGIN OLIVE OIL
¼ TSP. GROUND CUMIN
⅛ TSP. GROUND CORIANDER
¼ TSP. SALT
⅛ TSP. GROUND BLACK PEPPER
1½ CUPS RED LENTILS, COOKED
¼ SWEET ONION, ROUGHLY CUT
2 CLOVES GARLIC, PEELED
½ JALAPEÑO PEPPER, SEEDED, ROUGHLY CUT
1 OR 2 INDIAN NAAN BREADS, TORN INTO BITE-SIZED PIECES

Place the juice, oil, cumin, coriander, salt and pepper in the 40 oz. Processing Bowl. Pulse 3 times. Add the lentils, onion, garlic and pepper. Pulse until smooth. Chill very well before serving with the bread. Serves 3 to 4.

CAL 206, FAT 6G, SAT FAT 0G, CHOL 0MG, SODIUM 148MG,
CARBS 30G, PROTEIN 7G, FIBER 6G, CALCIUM 20MG, POTASSIUM 343MG

FIRE-ROASTED TOMATO SALSA WITH TORTILLA CHIPS

14.5 OZ. CAN FIRE-ROASTED TOMATOES, WITH JUICE
½ SMALL RED ONION, PEELED, ROUGHLY CUT
4 CLOVES GARLIC, PEELED
½ TSP. SALT
¼ TSP. GROUND BLACK PEPPER
¼ TSP. GROUND CUMIN
¼ CUP FRESH CILANTRO LEAVES
2 TBSP. FRESH LIME JUICE
6 OZ. BAKED TORTILLA CHIPS

Place all ingredients, except the chips, in the 40 oz. Processing Bowl and pulse until fairly smooth. Taste and adjust seasonings, as desired. Serve right away with tortilla chips or refrigerate for up to 2 days. Makes about 1½ cups.

CAL 110, FAT 1G, SAT FAT 0G, CHOL 0MG, SODIUM 305MG,
CARBS 22G, PROTEIN 2G, FIBER 2G, CALCIUM 55MG, POTASSIUM 229MG

TOMATILLO SALSA VERDE

1 LB. GREEN TOMATILLOS, HUSKS, SEEDS AND PULP REMOVED
1 SERRANO CHILE PEPPER, SEEDED, ROUGHLY CUT
½ CUP WHITE ONION, ROUGHLY CUT
¼ CUP FRESH CILANTRO LEAVES
1½ TBSP. FRESH LIME JUICE
¼ TSP. SUGAR
½ TSP. SALT
4 WHOLE WHEAT TORTILLAS, TORN AND BROILED UNTIL CRISPY

Place the tomatillos in a medium saucepan and cover with water. Bring to a boil on high heat. When the water boils, reduce the heat and simmer for 5 minutes. Drain. Cool slightly and place in the 40 oz. Processing Bowl. Add the remaining ingredients, except the tortillas, and pulse until almost smooth. Serve with the tortilla crisps. Makes 4 servings.

CAL 171, FAT 5G, SAT FAT 1G, CHOL 0MG, SODIUM 809MG,
CARBS 97G, PROTEIN 5G, FIBER 3G, CALCIUM 51MG, POTASSIUM 147MG

THAI LETTUCE WRAPS
WITH PEANUT DIPPING SAUCE

PEANUT SAUCE:

2 TSP. FRESH GINGER, ROUGHLY CHOPPED
½ CUP WATER
1 TBSP. FISH SAUCE (OPTIONAL)
1 TBSP. RICE WINE VINEGAR
¼ CUP CREAMY PEANUT BUTTER
1 TBSP. SUGAR
¼ CUP HOISIN SAUCE
1 TBSP. FRESH CILANTRO LEAVES (OPTIONAL)

LETTUCE WRAPS:

2 LARGE BONELESS, SKINLESS CHICKEN BREASTS, COOKED, SLICED INTO THIN STRIPS
10 LARGE BUTTER LETTUCE LEAVES
¼ LB. VERMICELLI RICE NOODLES, COOKED AND COOLED
1 LARGE CARROT, PEELED AND SHREDDED
½ CUP FRESH CILANTRO LEAVES, ROUGHLY CHOPPED

Place all of the peanut sauce ingredients in the 16 oz. Single Serve Cup and pulse until very smooth. Pour into a small bowl and set aside. On a large serving platter, place the following ingredients in separate sections: chicken strips, butter lettuce leaves, rice noodles, shredded carrot and cilantro leaves. To assemble, fill the lettuce leaves with equal portions of chicken, noodles, carrots, and cilantro. Roll up and serve right away with the peanut dipping sauce. Makes 10 lettuce wraps.

SAUCE: **CAL 135, FAT 7G, SAT FAT 1G, CHOL 0MG, SODIUM 704MG, CARBS 15G, PROTEIN 4G, FIBER 1G, CALCIUM 15MG, POTASSIUM 129MG**

WRAPS: **CAL 75, FAT 0G, SAT FAT 0G, CHOL 18MG, SODIUM 33MG, CARBS 9G, PROTEIN 8G, FIBER 1G, CALCIUM 14MG, POTASSIUM 105MG**

DUXELLE CUCUMBER CUPS

1 LB. FRESH CREMINI MUSHROOMS, TRIMMED
1 CLOVE GARLIC, PEELED
1 TSP. FRESH THYME LEAVES
1 TSP. LEMON ZEST
1 TBSP. EXTRA VIRGIN OLIVE OIL
½ TSP. SALT
¼ TSP. GROUND BLACK PEPPER
2 SEEDLESS, THIN-SKINNED ENGLISH CUCUMBERS
¼ CUP CRÈME FRAICHE (OR USE SOUR CREAM, IF DESIRED)
PARSLEY FOR GARNISH (OPTIONAL)

Place the mushrooms, garlic, thyme and lemon zest in the 40 oz. Processing Bowl and pulse until the mixture is chunky. In a large pan over medium-high heat, sauté the mushroom mixture in the olive oil for about 5 minutes, allowing the excess liquid to cook off. Add salt and pepper and let cool.

Meanwhile, peel the cucumber partially, so it still has strips of skin. Trim the ends off the cucumbers and cut each cucumber into slices 1-inch thick. Scoop out the center of each slice with a melon baller, forming a cup of flesh. Fill the cucumber cup with 1 teaspoon of the mushroom mixture. Top each with a dollop of crème fraiche and garnish with parsley leaves. Makes 16 appetizers.

CAL 91, FAT 3G, SAT FAT 1G, CHOL 3MG, SODIUM 1216MG, CARBS 7G, PROTEIN 2G, FIBER 2G, CALCIUM 18MG, POTASSIUM 277MG

MELON CUCUMBER SALSA

½ HONEYDEW MELON, PEELED, ROUGHLY CUT
½ CUCUMBER, PEELED, ROUGHLY CUT
1¼ CUPS FRESH DILL, ROUGHLY CUT
½ RIPE TOMATO, ROUGHLY CUT
½ SWEET ONION, PEELED, ROUGHLY CUT
½ TSP. LEMON JUICE

Place all ingredients in the 40 oz. Processing Bowl and pulse a few times until evenly chopped. Makes about 2 cups.

CAL 21, FAT 0G, SAT FAT 0G, CHOL 0MG, SODIUM 8MG,
CARBS 5G, PROTEIN 0G, FIBER 0G, CALCIUM 6MG, POTASSIUM 160MG

BACON & CHEDDAR STUFFED BOULE

6 SLICES CRISP COOKED BACON, PLUS MORE FOR GARNISH
¼ RED ONION, PEELED, ROUGHLY CUT
1 SPRIG ROSEMARY, REMOVED FROM STALK, PLUS MORE FOR GARNISH
4 OZ. EXTRA SHARP CHEDDAR CHEESE, CUT INTO 1 OUNCE STICKS
1 TBSP. BALSAMIC VINEGAR
½ CUP LOW FAT PLAIN GREEK YOGURT
8 OZ. LOW FAT CREAM CHEESE
1 BOULE SOURDOUGH BREAD (ROUND BREAD LOAF)

Preheat the oven to 350°F.

Place all ingredients, except the bread, in the 40 oz. Processing Bowl and pulse until smooth. Slice off the top of the sourdough round and remove most of the bread center, reserving the bread inside. Fill the center of the boule with the dip and cover with the top slice. Wrap in foil and bake for 50 minutes. Unwrap and bake for an additional 10 minutes.

Cut the bread pieces into rough cubes and arrange around the boule. Garnish with additional bacon and rosemary. Serves 8.

CAL 253, FAT 7G, SAT FAT 3G, CHOL 13MG, SODIUM 563MG,
CARBS 33G, PROTEIN 15G, FIBER 1G, CALCIUM 96MG, POTASSIUM 90MG

BLUE CHEESE & WALNUT STUFFED PORTABELLO MUSHROOMS

¼ CUP TOASTED WALNUTS
3 LARGE PORTABELLO MUSHROOMS, CLEANED AND STEMS REMOVED
1 TBSP. EXTRA VIRGIN OLIVE OIL
½ TSP. SALT
¼ TSP. GROUND BLACK PEPPER
6 OZ. BLUE CHEESE, CRUMBLED
8 OZ. LOW FAT CREAM CHEESE, AT ROOM TEMPERATURE
3 TBSP. LOW FAT SOUR CREAM
2 TBSP. LOW FAT MILK

Preheat the broiler to High. Place the walnuts in the Single Serve Cup and pulse until chopped. Set aside. Brush the mushrooms with olive oil and place on the broiler pan. Season with salt and pepper. Broil for 5 to 6 minutes, turning once. Remove and set aside to cool.

Place the blue cheese, cream cheese, sour cream and milk in the 40 oz. Processing Bowl. Pulse until smooth. Spread the cheese mixture on the broiled mushrooms. Cut each mushroom into 6 wedges. Sprinkle with chopped walnuts and serve right away. Makes 18 appetizers.

CAL 91, FAT 7G, SAT FAT 4G, CHOL 16MG, SODIUM 239MG, CARBS 2G, PROTEIN 4G, FIBER 0G, CALCIUM 75MG, POTASSIUM 133MG

CHILLED JUMBO SHRIMP
WITH SWEET CHILI DIPPING SAUCE

1 LB. EXTRA LARGE SHRIMP, COOKED, SHELLED, DEVEINED, WITH TAILS
¼ CUP RICE WINE VINEGAR
2 TBSP. FISH SAUCE
¼ CUP HOT WATER
2 TBSP. SUGAR
1 TBSP. FRESH LIME JUICE
½ CLOVE GARLIC
1 TSP. ASIAN RED CHILI PASTE (SUCH AS SAMBAL)

Place the shrimp over ice in a serving bowl and keep well-chilled.

Combine all remaining ingredients in the Single Serve Cup and pulse until smooth. Serve the shrimp with the sauce right away. Chill any leftovers. Serves 3 to 4.

CAL 54, FAT 0G, SAT FAT 0G, CHOL 43MG, SODIUM 753MG,
CARBS 7G, PROTEIN 5G, FIBER 0G, CALCIUM 16MG, POTASSIUM 78MG

CRUDITES
WITH COOL ARTICHOKE-SPINACH DIP

COOL ARTICHOKE-SPINACH DIP:

8 OZ. LOW FAT CREAM CHEESE, AT ROOM TEMPERATURE
¼ CUP LOW FAT MILK
14 OZ. CAN ARTICHOKE HEARTS IN WATER, DRAINED AND ROUGHLY CHOPPED
1 CUP FRESH SPINACH LEAVES, WASHED AND DRAINED, STEMS REMOVED
3 GREEN ONIONS, ROUGHLY CUT
1 TBSP. FRESH LEMON JUICE
¼ CUP PARMESAN CHEESE, GRATED

CRUDITES:

BROCCOLI FLORETS
CARROT STICKS
RED PEPPER STRIPS
CELERY OR JICAMA STICKS

Place the cream cheese and milk in the 40 oz. Processing Bowl. Pulse until smooth. Add the remaining ingredients and pulse again until smooth. Spoon into a serving bowl. Serve with the crudités right away or chill until serving. Serves 8.

CAL 100, FAT 6G, SAT FAT 4G, CHOL 19MG, SODIUM 91MG, CARBS 6G, PROTEIN 2G, FIBER 1G, CALCIUM 70MG, POTASSIUM 101MG

SALSA GUACAMOLE

1/4 RED ONION, PEELED, ROUGHLY CUT
½ JALAPEÑO PEPPER, SEEDED, ROUGHLY CUT
1 LARGE TOMATO, QUARTERED
¼ CUP FRESH CILANTRO, LOOSELY PACKED
½ YELLOW PEPPER, SEEDED, ROUGHLY CUT
¼ TSP. RED PEPPER FLAKES
2 LIMES, JUICED
2 RIPE AVOCADOS, PITTED, PEELED, ROUGHLY CUT

Place all ingredients in the 40 oz. Processing Bowl. Pulse quickly three to six times to rough chop or pulse continuously for creamy texture. Makes about 2 cups.

CAL 125, FAT 10G, SAT FAT 1G, CHOL 0MG, SODIUM 7MG,
CARBS 10G, PROTEIN 2G, FIBER 5G, CALCIUM 14MG, POTASSIUM 422MG

GREEN GODDESS DIP
WITH TENDER-CRISP GREEN BEANS

1 CUP LOW FAT PLAIN GREEK YOGURT
2 RIPE AVOCADOS, PEELED AND PIT REMOVED
2 GREEN ONIONS, COARSELY CHOPPED
¼ CUP FRESH FLAT-LEAF PARSLEY
¼ CUP FRESH BASIL LEAVES
1 TBSP. FRESH TARRAGON LEAVES
3 TBSP. FRESH LEMON JUICE
½ TSP. SALT
¼ TSP. GROUND BLACK PEPPER
1 LB. FRESH GREEN BEANS, STEAMED AND CHILLED

Place all the ingredients, except the beans, in the 40 oz. Processing Bowl and pulse until very smooth. Spoon the dip into a serving bowl and serve right away with the green beans for dipping. Serves 6.

CAL 162, FAT 10G, SAT FAT 2G, CHOL 2MG, SODIUM 219MG,
CARBS 13G, PROTEIN 7G, FIBER 7G, CALCIUM 86MG, POTASSIUM 505MG

JAPANESE PORK POTSTICKERS WITH SPICY ASIAN DIPPING SAUCE

1 CLOVE GARLIC, PEELED
½-INCH GINGER, PEELED
2 GREEN ONIONS, ROUGHLY CUT
1 MEDIUM CARROT, PEELED, QUARTERED
1 CUP CABBAGE, FINELY SHREDDED
1 EGG
½ LB. GROUND EXTRA-LEAN PORK
36 GYOZA WRAPPERS (IN THE ASIAN FOODS AISLE)
2 TBSP. WATER
1 TBSP. CANOLA OIL

Place the garlic, ginger, onions and carrot in the 40 oz. Processing Bowl. Pulse until finely chopped. Place in a large bowl and add the cabbage, egg and ground pork. Toss lightly until combined. In the middle of one wrapper, mound about 2 teaspoons of the filling. Brush the edges of the wrapper with the water and seal the edges to form half-moons.

Heat the oil in a sauté pan over medium-high heat. Place some of the potstickers flat side down, not touching, in the pan and cook until they brown on the bottom. With pan cover in one hand, add ½ cup water and immediately cover. Let steam for 5 minutes, checking to add water if needed. Let the water fully evaporate so that the potstickers can crisp up again. Repeat process with remaining potstickers. Serves 18; 2 potstickers per serving.

CAL 53, FAT 2G, SAT FAT 0G, CHOL 6MG, SODIUM 122MG,
CARBS 7G, PROTEIN 2G, FIBER 0G, CALCIUM 2MG, POTASSIUM 0MG

CRISP CAULIFLOWER
WITH LEMON TAHINI SAUCE

½ CUP TAHINI (SESAME BUTTER)
¼ CUP FRESH LEMON JUICE
2 CLOVES GARLIC, PEELED
2 TBSP. EXTRA VIRGIN OLIVE OIL
½ TSP. SALT
1 TBSP. WATER
1 HEAD FRESH CAULIFLOWER, CUT INTO SMALL FLORETS, CHILLED

Place all ingredients, except the cauliflower, in the 40 oz. Processing Bowl and pulse until smooth. Add water as needed to thin the sauce to desired consistency. Place in a serving bowl and surround with the fresh cauliflower for dipping. Serves 4 to 6.

CAL 176, FAT 15G, SAT FAT 2G, CHOL 0MG, SODIUM 36MG,
CARBS 92G, PROTEIN 5G, FIBER 3G, CALCIUM 48MG, POTASSIUM 377MG

PARMESAN WHOLE WHEAT BREAD CRUMBS

4 OZ. PARMESAN CHEESE, CUT INTO 4 PIECES
1 TBSP. HERBS DE PROVENCE OR ITALIAN SEASONING, TO TASTE
3 SLICES WHOLE GRAIN BREAD, TORN INTO 4 PIECES

Place all ingredients in the 40 oz. Processing Bowl and pulse until even crumbs form. Makes about 1 cup.

CAL 66, FAT 3G, SAT FAT 2G, CHOL 8MG, SODIUM 171MG, CARBS 6G, PROTEIN 5G, FIBER 5G, CALCIUM 106MG, POTASSIUM 22MG

CLASSIC MARGARITA – P. 61
SUMMER PEACH BELLINI – P. 62
APRICOT MOJITO CRUSH – P. 63
CRANBERRY COSMO FREEZE – P. 64
BLUEBERRY CAIPIROSKA – P. 65
HONEYDEW MELON GIMLET – P. 66
RIPE PLUM PARADISE – P. 67
PERFECT PINA COLADA – P. 68

CHAPTER THREE :: COCKTAILS & PARTY DRINKS

SAIGON BY NIGHT – P. 69
GRANNY'S APPLE MARTINI – P. 70
HARD APPLE POMEGRANATE CIDER – P. 71
REFRESHING CUCUMBER & MINT CHAMPAGNE COCKTAILS – P. 72
TROPICAL SUNSET SPARKLER – P. 73
BLACKBERRY GIN TWIST – P. 74
HARD RASPBERRY & MINT LEMONADE – P. 75

BLUEBERRY CAIPIROSKA – P. 65

APRICOT MOJITO CRUSH – P. 63

REFRESHING CUCUMBER & MINT CHAMPAGNE COCKTAILS – P. 72

CRANBERRY COSMO FREEZE – P. 64

HONEYDEW MELON GIMLET – P. 66

HARD APPLE POMEGRANATE CIDER – P. 71

TROPICAL SUNSET SPARKLER – P. 73

CLASSIC MARGARITA P. 61

CLASSIC MARGARITA

½ CUP FRESH LIME JUICE
2 TBSP. FRESH ORANGE JUICE
2 TBSP. FRESH LEMON JUICE
4 OZ. ORANGE LIQUEUR
4 OZ. TEQUILA
1 TBSP. SUGAR OR AGAVE NECTAR (OPTIONAL)
16 TO 18 ICE CUBES

Place all ingredients in the 40 oz. Processing Bowl and pulse until smooth. Taste and add the sugar or nectar if you like a sweeter flavor. Serve immediately. Serves 3-4.

CAL 182, FAT 0G, SAT FAT 0G, CHOL 0MG, SODIUM 1MG,
CARBS 13G, PROTEIN 0G, FIBER 0G, CALCIUM 9MG, POTASSIUM 107MG

SUMMER PEACH BELLINI

2 RIPE PEACHES, PEELED AND PITTED
6 OZ. PEACH SCHNAPPS
10 OZ. PROSECCO, CHILLED
14-16 ICE CUBES

Place all ingredients in the 40 oz. Processing Bowl and pulse until icy and smooth. Serve in champagne glasses. Serves 4.

CAL 292, FAT 0G, SAT FAT 0G, CHOL 0MG, SODIUM 0MG,
CARBS 24G, FIBER 1G, PROTEIN 0G, CALCIUM 6MG, POTASSIUM 186MG

APRICOT MOJITO CRUSH

4 RIPE APRICOTS, PEELED AND PITTED
1 TBSP. BLACKSTRAP MOLASSES
1 TBSP. WARM WATER
6 MINT LEAVES, PLUS EXTRA FOR GARNISH
8 OZ. WHITE RUM
4 OZ. CLUB SODA
14-16 ICE CUBES

Place the apricots, molasses and water in the 40 oz. Processing Bowl and pulse until smooth. Spoon equally into 4 glasses and set aside.

Place the remaining ingredients in the 40 oz. Processing Bowl and pulse until icy and smooth. Pour over the apricot crush and serve right away. Garnish with mint, if desired. Serves 4.

CAL 192, FAT 0G, SAT FAT 0G, CHOL 0MG, SODIUM 25MG, CARBS 16G, PROTEIN 0G, FIBER 1G, CALCIUM 175MG, POTASSIUM 592MG

CRANBERRY COSMO FREEZE

½ CUP FRESH CRANBERRIES, WASHED
½ CUP CRANBERRY JUICE
2 OZ. TRIPLE SEC
4 OZ. VODKA, CHILLED

In advance, place the cranberries and juice in the 40 oz. Processing Bowl and pulse until smooth. Spoon the mixture into ice cube trays and freeze until ice cubes are formed.

Place the cranberry ice cubes and the remaining ingredients in the 40 oz. Processing Bowl. Pulse until smooth. Serve right away in chilled martini glasses. Serves 4.

CAL 293, FAT 0G, SAT FAT 0G, CHOL 0MG, SODIUM 18MG,
CARBS 7G, PROTEIN 6G, FIBER 0G, CALCIUM 0MG, POTASSIUM 26MG

BLUEBERRY CAIPIROSKA

1 CUP FRESH BLUEBERRIES, WASHED

8 OZ. VODKA

16 ICE CUBES

8 LARGE MINT LEAVES FOR GARNISH

Place all ingredients in the 40 oz. Processing Bowl and pulse until smooth. Serves 4.

CAL 161, FAT 0G, SAT FAT 0G, CHOL 0MG, SODIUM 1MG,
CARBS 4G, PROTEIN 0G, FIBER 1G, CALCIUM 2MG, POTASSIUM 23MG

HONEYDEW MELON GIMLET

1 CUP HONEYDEW MELON, IN CHUNKS
2 TSP. FRESH LIME JUICE
8 OZ. DRY GIN
4 SLICES FRESH LIME (OPTIONAL)
ICE CUBES

Place the melon, juice and gin in the 40 oz. Processing Bowl and pulse until smooth. Strain before serving, if desired. Pour over ice cubes and garnish with lime slices. Serves 4.

CAL 146, FAT 0G, SAT FAT 0G, CHOL 0MG, SODIUM 9MG,
CARBS 6G, PROTEIN 1G, FIBER 1G, CALCIUM 13MG, POTASSIUM 174MG

RIPE PLUM PARADISE

1 FRESH, RIPE PLUM, PITTED
4 OZ. PLUM BRANDY
1 OZ. ORANGE LIQUEUR
8 OZ. DARK RUM
ICE CUBES

Place the plum, brandy, liqueur and rum in the 40 oz. Processing Bowl and pulse until smooth. Pour over the ice cubes before serving. Serves 3 to 4.

CAL 231, FAT 0G, SAT FAT 0G, CHOL 0MG, SODIUM 1MG,
CARBS 7G, PROTEIN 4G, FIBER 0G, CALCIUM 2MG, POTASSIUM 55MG

PERFECT PINA COLADA

1 CUP FRESH PINEAPPLE JUICE
1 CUP PINEAPPLE SORBET
½ CUP LIGHT COCONUT MILK
4 OZ. WHITE RUM
PINEAPPLE WEDGES (OPTIONAL)
ICE CUBES

Place all the ingredients, except the pineapple wedges, in the 40 oz. Processing Bowl and pulse until smooth. Pour over ice cubes into cocktail glasses and garnish with a wedge of fresh pineapple. Serves 4.

CAL 294, FAT 3G, SAT FAT 0G, CHOL 0MG, SODIUM 13MG,
CARBS 35G, PROTEIN 0G, FIBER 0G, CALCIUM 9MG, POTASSIUM 90MG

SAIGON BY NIGHT

2 CUPS VANILLA ICE CREAM
½ CUP COLD ESPRESSO COFFEE
2 OZ. COFFEE LIQUEUR

Place the ingredients in the 40 oz. Processing Bowl and pulse until smooth. Serves 4.

CAL 249, FAT 11G, SAT FAT 7G, CHOL 78MG, SODIUM 54MG,
CARBS 27G, PROTEIN 4G, FIBER 2G, CALCIUM 113MG, POTASSIUM 158MG

GRANNY'S APPLE MARTINI

1 GRANNY SMITH APPLE, PEELED, CORED, ROUGHLY CUT
8 OZ. VODKA, CHILLED
3 OZ. CALVADOS
ICE CUBES
APPLE PEEL FOR GARNISH (OPTIONAL)

Place the apple in the 40 oz. Processing Bowl and pulse until smooth. Add the remaining ingredients and pulse again. Strain before serving, if desired.

Fill 4 martini glasses with ice cubes and pour the apple martinis equally into each. Garnish with apple peel, if desired. Serve immediately. Serves 4.

CAL 248, FAT 0G, SAT FAT 0G, CHOL 0MG, SODIUM 2MG, CARBS 10G, PROTEIN 0G, FIBER 2G, CALCIUM 5MG, POTASSIUM 82MG

HARD APPLE POMEGRANATE CIDER

1 RIPE RED DELICIOUS APPLE, CORED, ROUGHLY CUT
8 OZ. APPLE BRANDY
½ CUP POMEGRANATE JUICE
1 CUP APPLE CIDER
2 CINNAMON STICKS

Place the apple in the 40 oz. Processing Bowl and pulse until smooth. Add the brandy, juice and cider and pulse again until smooth. Strain, if desired.

Pour the cider into a large saucepan and add the cinnamon sticks. Heat on medium-low until simmering, stirring occasionally. Remove the cinnamon sticks and ladle into four heatproof mugs. Serve right away. Serves 4.

CAL 184, FAT 0G, SAT FAT 0G, CHOL 0MG, SODIUM 30MG,
CARBS 32G, PROTEIN 0G, FIBER 0G, CALCIUM 61MG, POTASSIUM 339MG

REFRESHING CUCUMBER & MINT CHAMPAGNE COCKTAILS

1 SMALL CUCUMBER, PEELED, QUARTERED
6 LARGE MINT LEAVES
2 TBSP. RAW, UNFILTERED HONEY
2 OZ. MIDORI
12 OZ. DRY CHAMPAGNE, CHILLED

Place the cucumber, mint leaves and honey in the 40 oz. Processing Bowl and pulse until smooth. Add the Midori and champagne and pulse again. Strain and pour into champagne glasses. Serve right away. Serves 4.

CAL 137, FAT 0G, SAT FAT 0G, CHOL 0MG, SODIUM 1MG,
CARBS 8G, PROTEIN 1G, FIBER 1G, CALCIUM 7MG, POTASSIUM 71MG

TROPICAL SUNSET SPARKLER

20 ICE CUBES
½ CUP ORANGE JUICE
½ CUP PINEAPPLE JUICE
12 OZ. PROSECCO OR CHAMPAGNE
4 TBSP. GRENADINE
4 FRESH SWEET CHERRIES

Place the ice cubes in the 40 oz. Processing Bowl. Pulse until completely smooth. Divide the powdered ice evenly among four cocktail glasses.

Place the orange juice, pineapple juice, and Prosecco in the 40 oz. Processing Bowl and pulse until blended. Pour equally over the ice. Do not stir or mix. Drizzle 1 tablespoon of grenadine over the top of each cocktail and top with a cherry.

CAL 262, FAT 0G, SAT FAT 0G, CHOL 0MG, SODIUM 10MG,
CARBS 45G, PROTEIN 2G, FIBER 0G, CALCIUM 32MG, POTASSIUM 422MG

BLACKBERRY GIN TWIST

8 OZ. GIN
4 OZ. GINGER BEER
1 CUP FRESH, RIPE BLACKBERRIES, RINSED
14 TO 16 ICE CUBES
BLACKBERRIES FOR GARNISH (OPTIONAL)

Place all ingredients, except the garnish, in the 40 oz. Processing Bowl and pulse until smooth. Spoon into cocktail glasses and garnish each with a blackberry. Serve right away. Serves 4.

CAL 191, FAT 0G, SAT FAT 0G, CHOL 0MG, SODIUM 1MG, CARBS 17G, PROTEIN 0G, FIBER 2G, CALCIUM 8MG, POTASSIUM 47MG

HARD RASPBERRY & MINT LEMONADE

8 OZ. VODKA
8 OZ. CLUB SODA
½ CUP LEMONADE
½ CUP FRESH RASPBERRIES, RINSED
2 TBSP. POWDERED SUGAR
4 MINT LEAVES
ICE CUBES

Place all the ingredients, except the ice cubes, in the 40 oz. Processing Bowl and pulse until blended. Fill 4 cocktail glasses with ice cubes and pour the lemonade over each. Serve right away. Serves 4.

CAL 190, FAT 0G, SAT FAT 0G, CHOL 0MG, SODIUM 10MG,
CARBS 12G, PROTEIN 0G, FIBER 0G, CALCIUM 5MG, POTASSIUM 35MG

STRAWBERRY BANANA SMOOTHIE – P. 83
EMERALD GREEN ELIXIR – P. 84
BLUEBERRY BLAST – P. 85
POMEGRANATE POWER SMOOTHIE – P. 86
MANGO LASSI – P. 87
AVOCADO SHAKE – P. 88
DANDY GREEN MACHINE – P. 89
SWEET CHERRY SMOOTHIE – P. 90
KALE & DATE SMOOTHIE – P. 91
PEANUT BUTTER CHOCOLATE SMOOTHIE – P. 92
GALA APPLE CELEBRATION – P. 93
CARROT PROTEIN POWER – P. 94
VITAMIN C CUCUMBER BLAST – P. 95

CHAPTER FOUR :: SMOOTHIES & JUICES

DETOX ANTIOXIDANT JUICE – P. 96
RAINBOW JUICE – P. 97
VEGGIE FUSION – P. 98
SUMMER BERRY SENSATION – P. 99
GREEN PEAR SMOOTHIE – P. 100
PINEAPPLE PAPAYA SMOOTHIE – P. 101
FRESH CITRUS SQUEEZE – P. 102
QUICK ORANGESICLE – P. 103
PUMPKIN GINGER SMOOTHIE – P. 104
CARROT APPLE REFRESHER – P. 105
GARDEN VEGGIES IN A GLASS – P. 106
RED GRAPE SQUEEZE – P. 107
ALMOND & DARK MOLASSES DREAM – P. 108
GREEN TEA FREEZE – P. 109
WATERMELON & LIME SMOOTHIE – P. 110
MOCHA FREEZE – P. 111

CARROT APPLE REFRESHER – P.105

BLUEBERRY BLAST – P. 85

GARDEN VEGGIES IN A GLASS– P. 106

PEANUT BUTTER CHOCOLATE SMOOTHIE – P. 92

WATERMELON & LIME SMOOTHIE – P. 110

ALMOND & DARK MOLASSES DREAM – P. 108

STRAWBERRY BANANA SMOOTHIE

½ CUP APPLE JUICE
½ CUP LOW FAT PLAIN YOGURT
¾ CUP FRESH STRAWBERRIES, STEMMED AND HULLED
½ BANANA, PEELED
5 TO 6 ICE CUBES

Place all ingredients in the Single Serve Cup. Pulse until smooth. Serve right away.

CAL 224, FAT 2G, SAT FAT 1G, CHOL 7MG, SODIUM 19MG, CARBS 45G, PROTEIN 8G, FIBER 4G, CALCIUM 250MG, POTASSIUM 664MG

EMERALD GREEN ELIXIR

½ CUP WHITE GRAPE JUICE
½ SMALL BANANA, PEELED
½ CUP BABY SPINACH LEAVES
1 KIWI, PEELED
2 TSP. RAW, UNFILTERED HONEY
5 TO 6 ICE CUBES

Place all ingredients in the Single Serve Cup and pulse until smooth. Serve right away.

CAL 220, FAT 0G, SAT FAT 0G, CHOL 0MG, SODIUM 25MG,
CARBS 51G, PROTEIN 2G, FIBER 4G, CALCIUM 44MG, POTASSIUM 535MG

BLUEBERRY BLAST

½ CUP WHITE GRAPE JUICE
½ CUP LOW FAT PLAIN YOGURT
½ BANANA, PEELED
½ CUP FRESH OR FROZEN WILD BLUEBERRIES, RINSED
8 ICE CUBES

Place all ingredients in the Single Serve Cup and pulse until smooth.

CAL 252, FAT 2G, SAT FAT 1G, CHOL 7MG, SODIUM 97MG, CARBS 54G, PROTEIN 8G, FIBER 4G, CALCIUM 231MG, POTASSIUM 556MG

POMEGRANATE POWER SMOOTHIE

½ CUP LOW FAT PLAIN YOGURT
½ CUP POMEGRANATE JUICE
½ CUP FROZEN BLUEBERRIES
1 TBSP. RAW, UNFILTERED HONEY

Place all ingredients in the Single Serve Cup and pulse until smooth.

CAL 223, FAT 2G, SAT FAT 1G, CHOL 7MG, SODIUM 118MG,
CARBS 50G, PROTEIN 7G, FIBER 2G, CALCIUM 239MG, POTASSIUM 497MG

MANGO LASSI

½ CUP MANGO CHUNKS, FROZEN
½ CUP LOW FAT PLAIN YOGURT
¼ CUP MANGO JUICE OR MILK
1 TSP. RAW, UNFILTERED HONEY
PINCH GROUND CARDAMOM

Place all ingredients in the Single Serve Cup and pulse until smooth.

CAL 225, FAT 2G, SAT FAT 1G, CHOL 7MG, SODIUM 92MG,
CARBS 47G, PROTEIN 6G, FIBER 2G, CALCIUM 233MG, POTASSIUM 429MG

AVOCADO SHAKE

½ RIPE AVOCADO, PITTED AND PEELED
½ CUP LOW FAT MILK
1 TBSP. RAW, UNFILTERED HONEY
8 ICE CUBES

Place all ingredients in the Single Serve Cup and pulse until smooth. Serve at once.

CAL 306, FAT 16G, SAT FAT 3G, CHOL 6MG, SODIUM 483MG, CARBS 12G, PROTEIN 16G, FIBER 7G, CALCIUM 82MG, POTASSIUM 595MG

DANDY GREEN MACHINE

½ CUP APPLE JUICE
½ CUP SWISS CHARD, RINSED, ROUGHLY TORN
½ BANANA, PEELED
2 TBSP. GOJI BERRIES
6 TO 8 ICE CUBES

Place the ingredients in the Single Serve Cup and pulse until smooth. Serve right away.

CAL 220, FAT 1G, SAT FAT 0G, CHOL 0MG, SODIUM 115MG, CARBS 54G, PROTEIN 5G, FIBER 6G, CALCIUM 102MG, POTASSIUM 399MG

SWEET CHERRY SMOOTHIE

½ CUP LOW FAT MILK
½ CUP LOW FAT VANILLA YOGURT
½ CUP FRESH SWEET CHERRIES, PITTED
(OR USE FROZEN CHERRIES, IF DESIRED)
½ BANANA, PEELED
5 TO 6 ICE CUBES

Place all ingredients in the Single Serve Cup and pulse until smooth.

CAL 239, FAT 2G, SAT FAT 2G, CHOL 10MG, SODIUM 134MG,
CARBS 46G, PROTEIN 10G, FIBER 12G, CALCIUM 344MG, POTASSIUM 808MG

KALE & DATE SMOOTHIE

¾ CUP FRESH ORANGE JUICE
½ CUP NONFAT VANILLA YOGURT
½ BANANA, PEELED
½ CUP FRESH KALE, TIGHTLY PACKED
1 DATE, PITTED
5 TO 6 ICE CUBES

Place all ingredients in the Single Serve Cup. Pulse until smooth. Serve right away.

CAL 363, FAT 0G, SAT FAT 0G, CHOL 3MG, SODIUM 101MG,
CARBS 87G, PROTEIN 9G, FIBER 6G, CALCIUM 299MG, POTASSIUM 1052MG

PEANUT BUTTER CHOCOLATE SMOOTHIE

¼ CUP LOW FAT MILK

2 TBSP. CREAMY PEANUT BUTTER

¾ CUP LOW FAT VANILLA FROZEN YOGURT

1 OZ. DARK CHOCOLATE

Place all ingredients in the Single Serve Cup and pulse until smooth. Serve right away.

CAL 395, FAT 18G, SAT FAT 7G, CHOL 5MG, SODIUM 239MG,
CARBS 61G, PROTEIN 15G, FIBER 10G, CALCIUM 438MG, POTASSIUM 204MG

GALA APPLE CELEBRATION

½ CUP APPLE JUICE
½ RIPE GALA APPLE, CORED, ROUGHLY CUT
½ CUP COLLARD GREENS, RINSED, RIBS REMOVED
½ CUP NONFAT PLAIN YOGURT
PINCH GROUND CARDAMOM
5 TO 6 ICE CUBES

Place all ingredients in the Single Serve Cup and pulse until smooth. Strain before serving, if desired.

CAL 211, FAT 0G, SAT FAT 0G, CHOL 0MG, SODIUM 97MG, CARBS 47G, PROTEIN 7G, FIBER 4G, CALCIUM 216MG, POTASSIUM 195MG

CARROT PROTEIN POWER

½ CUP APPLE JUICE
½ SMALL CARROT, ROUGHLY CUT
¼ SMALL RIPE GRANNY SMITH APPLE
½ BANANA, PEELED
1 TBSP. WHEY PROTEIN POWDER
5 TO 6 ICE CUBES

Place all ingredients in the Single Serve Cup and pulse until smooth. Strain before serving, if desired.

CAL 271, FAT 2G, SAT FAT 1G, CHOL 60MG, SODIUM 93MG,
CARBS 46G, PROTEIN 19G, FIBER 5G, CALCIUM 17MG, POTASSIUM 640MG

VITAMIN C CUCUMBER BLAST

1 GRAPEFRUIT, PEELED AND QUARTERED
1 ORANGE, PEELED AND QUARTERED
¼ CUCUMBER, PEELED
2-3 ICE CUBES

Place all ingredients in the Single Serve Cup. Pulse until smooth.

CAL 150, FAT 0G, SAT FAT 0G, CHOL 0MG, SODIUM 1MG,
CARBS 38G, PROTEIN 3G, FIBER 6G, CALCIUM 90MG, POTASSIUM 661MG

DETOX ANTIOXIDANT JUICE

1 APPLE, CORED AND QUARTERED

½ STALK CELERY, QUARTERED

1 CUP GREEN TEA, COOLED

½ LEMON, JUICED

2-3 ICE CUBES

Place the ingredients in the Single Serve Cup. Pulse until smooth.

CAL 109, FAT 0G, SAT FAT 0G, CHOL 0MG, SODIUM 6MG,
CARBS 28G, PROTEIN 3G, FIBER 4G, CALCIUM 13MG, POTASSIUM 263MG

RAINBOW JUICE

4 LARGE STRAWBERRIES, STEMMED
¼ CUP PINEAPPLE, ROUGHLY CUT
½ CUP GREENS (USE SPINACH, COLLARD GREENS, DANDELION GREENS OR KALE)
⅓ CUP WATER
2-3 ICE CUBES

Place all ingredients in the Single Serve Cup. Pulse until smooth.

CAL 53, FAT 0G, SAT FAT 0G, CHOL 0MG, SODIUM 14MG, CARBS 12G, PROTEIN 1G, FIBER 3G, CALCIUM 58MG, POTASSIUM 268MG

VEGGIE FUSION

⅛ CUCUMBER, CUT INTO 2 WEDGES, 3 INCHES IN LENGTH
2 BABY CARROTS
1 SMALL STALK CELERY, CUT IN HALF TO 3 INCHES IN LENGTH
½ CUP SPINACH LEAVES, LIGHTLY PACKED
¼ RIPE TOMATO
7 RED OR GREEN SEEDLESS GRAPES
¼-⅓ CUP WATERMELON, CUT INTO CHUNKS
3-4 ORANGE SLICES, PEELED
2 FRESH STRAWBERRIES (OR USE FROZEN)
2-4 ICE CUBES

Place all the ingredients in the Single Serve Cup. Pulse until smooth.

CAL 42, FAT 0G, SAT FAT 0G, CHOL 0MG, SODIUM 32MG, CARBS 19G, PROTEIN 1G, FIBER 2G, CALCIUM 63MG, POTASSIUM 583MG

SUMMER BERRY SENSATION

½ CUP APPLE JUICE
½ CUP LOW FAT VANILLA FROZEN YOGURT
¼ CUP FROZEN RASPBERRIES
¼ CUP FROZEN BLUEBERRIES
¼ CUP FROZEN STRAWBERRIES

Place all ingredients in the Single Serve Cup and pulse until smooth. Serve right away.

CAL 266, FAT 3G, SAT FAT 2G, CHOL 10MG, SODIUM 66MG,
CARBS 55G, PROTEIN 11G, FIBER 5G, CALCIUM 202MG, POTASSIUM 173MG

GREEN PEAR SMOOTHIE

½ CUP BABY SPINACH LEAVES
½ RIPE BARTLETT PEAR, PEELED AND CORED
½ BANANA, PEELED
5 TO 6 ICE CUBES

Place all ingredients in the Single Serve Cup and pulse until smooth. Strain before serving, if desired. Serve right away.

CAL 104, FAT 0G, SAT FAT 0G, CHOL 0MG, SODIUM 14MG, CARBS 27G, PROTEIN 1G, FIBER 5G, CALCIUM 26MG, POTASSIUM 394MG

PINEAPPLE PAPAYA SMOOTHIE

¼ CUP PAPAYA JUICE
½ CUP FRESH PINEAPPLE, CUT INTO CHUNKS
½ CUP FRESH PAPAYA
½ CUP LOW FAT VANILLA YOGURT
5 TO 6 ICE CUBES

Place all ingredients in the Single Serve Cup and pulse until smooth.

CAL 191, FAT 1G, SAT FAT 1G, CHOL 5MG, SODIUM 79MG, CARBS 41G, PROTEIN 5G, FIBER 2G, CALCIUM 192MG, POTASSIUM 515MG

FRESH CITRUS SQUEEZE

¼ CUP FRESH ORANGE JUICE
½ CUP FRESH RED GRAPEFRUIT, PEELED, SEGMENTED
½ CUP FRESH ORANGE, PEELED, SEGMENTED
½ CUP LOW FAT PLAIN YOGURT
1 TSP. POWDERED SUGAR
6 ICE CUBES

Place all ingredients in the Single Serve Cup and pulse until smooth. Serve right away.

CAL 201, FAT 1G, SAT FAT 1G, CHOL 5MG, SODIUM 73MG, CARBS 45G, PROTEIN 2G, FIBER 2G, CALCIUM 196MG, POTASSIUM 521MG

QUICK ORANGESICLE

1 CUP LOW FAT VANILLA FROZEN YOGURT
¼ CUP ORANGE JUICE
½ CUP FRESH ORANGE, PEELED, SEGMENTED

Place all ingredients in the Single Serve Cup and pulse until smooth. Serve right away.

CAL 287, FAT 0G, SAT FAT 0G, CHOL 4MG, SODIUM 122MG, CARBS 64G, PROTEIN 1G, FIBER 3G, CALCIUM 76MG, POTASSIUM 763MG

PUMPKIN GINGER SMOOTHIE

½ CUP PUMPKIN PUREE
½ CUP ORANGE JUICE
½ CUP LOW FAT VANILLA YOGURT
⅛ TSP. FRESH GINGER
PINCH GROUND CINNAMON (OPTIONAL)
RAW, UNFILTERED HONEY (OPTIONAL)
5 TO 6 ICE CUBES

Place all ingredients in the Single Serve Cup and pulse until smooth.

CAL 364, FAT 0G, SAT FAT 0G, CHOL 4MG, SODIUM 403MG,
CARBS 84G, PROTEIN 3G, FIBER 11G, CALCIUM 72MG, POTASSIUM 705MG

CARROT APPLE REFRESHER

½ CUP CARROT JUICE
½ SMALL CARROT, PEELED, ROUGHLY CUT
½ SMALL RIPE GRANNY SMITH APPLE, PEELED, ROUGHLY CUT
¼ CUP LOW FAT PLAIN YOGURT
1 TSP. RAW, UNFILTERED HONEY (OR TO TASTE)
PINCH GROUND CLOVES
5 TO 6 ICE CUBES

Place all ingredients in the Single Serve Cup and pulse until smooth.

CAL 183, FAT 0G, SAT FAT 0G, CHOL 2MG, SODIUM 93MG, CARBS 26G, PROTEIN 1G, FIBER 3G, CALCIUM 41MG, POTASSIUM 388MG

GARDEN VEGGIES IN A GLASS

½ CUP APPLE JUICE
½ SMALL RIPE TOMATO, PEELED, CUT IN HALF
½ INNER STALK CELERY, WITH LEAVES
1 TBSP. FRESH FLAT-LEAF PARSLEY
½ GREEN ONION, ROUGHLY CUT
PINCH SALT
¼ TSP. GROUND BLACK PEPPER

Place all ingredients in the Single Serve Cup and pulse until smooth. Strain before serving, if desired.

CAL 78, FAT 0G, SAT FAT 0G, CHOL 0MG, SODIUM 165MG, CARBS 16G, PROTEIN 1G, FIBER 2G, CALCIUM 18MG, POTASSIUM 332MG

RED GRAPE SQUEEZE

1 CUP FROZEN, SEEDLESS RED GRAPES
½ CUP WHITE GRAPE JUICE
½ CUP LOW FAT VANILLA YOGURT

Place all ingredients in the Single Serve Cup and pulse until smooth.

CAL 192, FAT 0G, SAT FAT 0G, CHOL 2MG, SODIUM 28MG,
CARBS 29G, PROTEIN 0G, FIBER 0G, CALCIUM 8MG, POTASSIUM 319MG

ALMOND & DARK MOLASSES DREAM

¼ CUP ALMOND MILK
1 TSP. BLACKSTRAP MOLASSES
1 CUP LOW FAT VANILLA FROZEN YOGURT
¼ TSP. PURE ALMOND EXTRACT
(OPTIONAL)

Place all ingredients in the Single Serve Cup and pulse until smooth.

CAL 288, FAT 7G, SAT FAT 4G, CHOL 30MG, SODIUM 179MG,
CARBS 58G, PROTEIN 6G, FIBER 0G, CALCIUM 422MG, POTASSIUM 543MG

GREEN TEA FREEZE

½ CUP GREEN TEA, COOLED
1 CUP LOW FAT VANILLA FROZEN YOGURT
PINCH GROUND NUTMEG
PINCH GROUND CARDAMOM
5 TO 6 ICE CUBES

Place all ingredients in the Single Serve Cup and pulse until smooth.

CAL 240, FAT 6G, SAT FAT 4G, CHOL 30MG, SODIUM 130MG, CARBS 44G, PROTEIN 6G, FIBER 0G, CALCIUM 200MG

WATERMELON & LIME SMOOTHIE

¼ CUP WHITE GRAPE JUICE
1 CUP SEEDLESS WATERMELON CHUNKS, FROZEN
½ TSP. LIME ZEST (OPTIONAL)
1 TSP. RAW, UNFILTERED HONEY (OPTIONAL)

Place all ingredients in the Single Serve Cup and pulse until smooth. Serve right away.

CAL 141, FAT 0G, SAT FAT 0G, CHOL 0MG, SODIUM 7MG, CARBS 37G, PROTEIN 1G, FIBER 0G, CALCIUM 10MG, POTASSIUM 148MG

MOCHA FREEZE

½ CUP STRONG COFFEE, COOLED
½ CUP LOW FAT CHOCOLATE FROZEN YOGURT
1 OZ. DARK CHOCOLATE
5 TO 6 ICE CUBES

Place all ingredients in the Single Serve Cup and pulse until smooth. Serve right away.

CAL 318, FAT 13G, SAT FAT 7G, CHOL 17MG, SODIUM 85MG, CARBS 47G, PROTEIN 7G, FIBER 5G, CALCIUM 137MG, POTASSIUM 0MG

ISLAND BUTTERNUT SQUASH SOUP – P. 119
ROASTED VEGETABLE BISQUE – P. 120
COOL SUMMERTIME CORN & RED PEPPER SOUP – P. 121
WATERMELON MINT SOUP – P. 122
SPICED CARROT APPLE SOUP WITH TOASTED HAZELNUTS – P. 123
SPICY BLACK BEAN SOUP – P. 124
DUO TOMATO GAZPACHO – P. 125
SPRING ASPARAGUS SOUP WITH CRÈME FRAICHE – P. 126
ROASTED GARLIC & ROMA TOMATO SOUP – P. 127
HEARTY VEGETABLE SOUP – P. 128
SMOKED HAM, SWEET POTATO AND APPLE SOUP – P. 129
EAST INDIAN CURRIED CAULIFLOWER SOUP – P. 130
SPEEDY CHICKEN TORTILLA SOUP – P. 131
BABY SPINACH SALAD WITH CHAMPAGNE HONEY VINAIGRETTE – P. 132

CHAPTER FIVE :: SOUPS & SALADS

CRISP BROCCOLI RABE & BLACK OLIVE TAPENADE SALAD – P. 133
CHOPPED VEGETABLE SALAD WITH DIJON VINAIGRETTE – P. 134
SUPER GREEN SUNFLOWER SALAD – P. 135
BOK CHOY SALAD WITH CASHEW DRESSING – P. 136
ORANGE FENNEL SALAD – P. 137
MEXICAN CHICKEN SALAD WITH CHIPOTLE LIME DRESSING – P. 138
ASIAN SHRIMP SLAW WITH GINGER SESAME VINAIGRETTE – P. 139
BROCCOLI SALAD WITH ALMOND MISO DRESSING – P. 140
CHICKEN CAESAR SALAD – P. 141
APPLE, RED ONION & CRANBERRY SALAD WITH ALMOND VINAIGRETTE – P. 142
THREE BEAN SALAD WITH ITALIAN HERB VINAIGRETTE – P. 143
ARUGULA, NECTARINE & PECAN SALAD WITH BLUE CHEESE DRESSING – P. 144
WHEATBERRY SALAD WITH WALNUT SHALLOT VINAIGRETTE – P. 145
BRUSSELS SPROUT SALAD WITH MAPLE-MUSTARD DRESSING – P. 146
ALBACORE TUNA & DILL SALAD – P. 147

COOL SUMMERTIME CORN & RED PEPPER SOUP – P. 121

BOK CHOY SALAD WITH CASHEW DRESSING – P. 136

ASIAN SHRIMP SLAW WITH GINGER SESAME VINAIGRETTE – P. 139

BABY SPINACH SALAD WITH CHAMPAGNE HONEY VINAIGRETTE – P. 132

DUO TOMATO GAZPACHO – P. 125

ISLAND BUTTERNUT SQUASH SOUP – P. 119

ISLAND BUTTERNUT SQUASH SOUP

3 CLOVES GARLIC, PEELED
2 TBSP. FRESH GINGER, PEELED
1 JALAPEÑO PEPPER, SEEDED
1 MEDIUM YELLOW ONION, PEELED, ROUGHLY CUT
4 LBS. BUTTERNUT SQUASH, COOKED, CUBED AND COOLED
3 CUPS SODIUM-REDUCED CHICKEN OR VEGETABLE BROTH
1 TSP. SALT (OR TO TASTE)
1 TBSP. BROWN SUGAR (OPTIONAL)

Place the garlic, ginger, pepper and onion in the 40 oz. Processing Bowl and pulse until finely chopped. Set aside.

Working in batches, pulse the butternut squash in the 40 oz. Processing Bowl and add broth to create a pourable puree. Pour the pureed squash into a large saucepot and add the chopped vegetables. Repeat with the remaining squash. Slowly add the remaining broth, whisking together to combine. Season with salt and sugar as desired. Heat on medium until simmering and ready to serve, about 8 minutes. Serves 4.

CAL 70, FAT 0G, SAT FAT 0G, CHOL 0MG, SODIUM 999MG,
CARBS 15G, PROTEIN 3G, FIBER 3G, CALCIUM 65MG, POTASSIUM 518MG

ROASTED VEGETABLE BISQUE

6 CUPS ROASTED ROOT VEGETABLES (BROCCOLI, ASPARAGUS, SQUASH, SWEET POTATO, CAULIFLOWER, ETC.), COOLED
1 TBSP. FRESH CHIVES
1 TBSP . FLAT-LEAF PARSLEY
3 CUPS SODIUM-REDUCED CHICKEN OR VEGETABLE BROTH, DIVIDED
½ CUP LOW FAT MILK (OR CREAM, IF DESIRED)
1 TSP. SALT (OR TO TASTE)
1 TSP. GROUND BLACK PEPPER

Place about one-third of the vegetables and herbs in the 40 oz. Processing Bowl and add one-half cup of broth. Pulse until pureed and smooth. Spoon the puree into a saucepot and repeat with the remaining roasted vegetables and herbs.

Add the remaining broth and milk, mixing well, and heat on medium until just simmering. Season with salt and pepper to taste, and continue simmering for about 10 minutes. Serves 4.

CAL 115, FAT 1G, SAT FAT 0G, CHOL 1MG, SODIUM 886MG, CARBS 24G, PROTEIN 11G, FIBER 6G, CALCIUM 101MG, POTASSIUM 741MG

COOL SUMMERTIME CORN & RED PEPPER SOUP

½ MEDIUM YELLOW ONION, PEELED, ROUGHLY CUT
3 JARRED ROASTED RED PEPPERS
2 15 OZ. CANS CORN, DRAINED, DIVIDED
2 CUPS VEGETABLE BROTH, DIVIDED
1 CUP LOW FAT SOUR CREAM
1 TBSP. FRESH CILANTRO LEAVES

Place the onion, red peppers and one can of corn in the 40 oz. Processing Bowl and pulse until finely chopped. Add one-half of the vegetable broth and pulse again.

Pour the mixture into a large serving bowl and add the remaining corn, broth, sour cream and cilantro. Stir lightly until well-mixed and serve right away or chill until serving. Serves 4.

CAL 213, FAT 8G, SAT FAT 4G, CHOL 20MG, SODIUM 836MG,
CARBS 37G, PROTEIN 6G, FIBER 4G, CALCIUM 90MG, POTASSIUM 415MG

WATERMELON MINT SOUP

3½ CUPS WATERMELON, CUT INTO 1-INCH PIECES
1 TBSP. SUGAR
1 LEMON, JUICED
8 MINT LEAVES
1 SLICE FRESH GINGER, PEELED
⅛ CUP SPARKLING WATER

Place all ingredients in the 40 oz. Processing Bowl and pulse to blend until smooth. Serves 4.

CAL 52, FAT 0G, SAT FAT 0G, CHOL 0MG, SODIUM 5MG,
CARBS 13G, PROTEIN 1G, FIBER 0G, CALCIUM 10MG, POTASSIUM 151MG

SPICED CARROT APPLE SOUP WITH TOASTED HAZELNUTS

2 CUPS CARROTS, PEELED, ROUGHLY CUT
1 MEDIUM RIPE GALA APPLE, PEELED, ROUGHLY CUT
¼-INCH PIECE FRESH GINGER, PEELED
1 TSP. GROUND CINNAMON
3 CUPS REDUCED-SODIUM CHICKEN OR VEGETABLE BROTH
½ CUP HAZELNUTS, SKINS REMOVED
1 TBSP. BUTTER

Place the carrots in the 40 oz. Processing Bowl and pulse until finely chopped. Spoon the carrots into a saucepot and set aside. Place the apple, ginger and cinnamon in the Bowl and pulse until finely chopped. Add the mixture to the carrots in the saucepot. Add the broth to the carrot/apple mixture and heat on medium until warm and simmering, about 8 minutes.

Meanwhile, place the hazelnuts in the Bowl and pulse until chopped. Remove and sauté the nuts in the butter on medium heat until lightly toasted and fragrant, about 2 minutes. To serve, ladle the warm soup into bowls and top with the toasted hazelnuts. Serves 4.

CAL 132, FAT 7G, SAT FAT 2G, CHOL 8MG, SODIUM 481MG,
CARBS 14G, PROTEIN 4G, FIBER 4G, CALCIUM 47MG, POTASSIUM 457MG

SPICY BLACK BEAN SOUP

2 14 OZ. CANS BLACK BEANS, DRAINED
1 JALAPEÑO PEPPER, SEEDED, ROUGHLY CUT
1 RIPE TOMATO, ROUGHLY CUT
½ LIME, JUICED
¼ WHITE ONION, PEELED, ROUGHLY CUT
2 CLOVES GARLIC, PEELED
¼ RED PEPPER, SEEDED, ROUGHLY CUT
¼ CUP FRESH CILANTRO, LOOSELY PACKED
SALT AND PEPPER TO TASTE

Place all of the ingredients in the 40 oz. Processing Bowl and pulse until smooth. Heat briefly or serve at room temperature. Serves 4.

CAL 184, FAT 1G, SAT FAT 0G, CHOL 0MG, SODIUM 696MG,
CARBS 37G, PROTEIN 13G, FIBER 12G, CALCIUM 98MG, POTASSIUM 67MG

DUO TOMATO GAZPACHO

1 SLICE STALE WHITE BREAD, ROUGHLY TORN
6 PLUM TOMATOES, HALVED
1 MEDIUM SEEDLESS CUCUMBER, PEELED AND QUARTERED
1 BELL PEPPER, CORED AND SEEDED, QUARTERED
1 CLOVE GARLIC, PEELED
2 TBSP. RED WINE VINEGAR
1 TSP. SALT (OR TO TASTE)
½ TSP. GROUND BLACK PEPPER
1 CUP TOMATO JUICE (PLUS 1 CUP, TO TASTE)

Pulse the bread in the 40 oz. Processing Bowl until crumbed. Place in a large serving bowl. Place 3 tomatoes in the Bowl and pulse until smooth. Pour into the serving bowl with the crumbs. Repeat with the remaining tomatoes. Pulse the bell pepper and garlic and add to the tomatoes and crumbs.

Add the vinegar, salt and pepper to taste, plus the tomato juice to taste. Stir well and chill until serving. Serves 4.

CAL 55, FAT 0G, SAT FAT 0G, CHOL 0MG, SODIUM 954MG,
CARBS 12G, PROTEIN 3G, FIBER 2G, CALCIUM 35MG, POTASSIUM 467MG

SPRING ASPARAGUS SOUP WITH CRÈME FRAICHE

1 LARGE LEEK, GREEN LEAVES REMOVED
1 TBSP. EXTRA VIRGIN OLIVE OIL
1 LB. ASPARAGUS SPEARS, WOODY ENDS REMOVED
2¼ CUPS REDUCED SODIUM CHICKEN OR VEGETABLE BROTH, DIVIDED
1½ CUPS SPRING PEAS (FRESH OR FROZEN)
1 CUP LOW FAT PLAIN YOGURT
3 FRESH MINT LEAVES
½ CUP CRÈME FRAICHE FOR GARNISH (OPTIONAL)

Place the leek in the Single Serve Cup and pulse until chopped. Heat the oil on medium-high in a large saucepot and sauté the leek for 5 minutes. Add the asparagus spears and 1 cup broth and bring to a boil. Reduce to a simmer, cover, and cook about 3 minutes. Add the peas. After another minute, remove from heat and let cool.

Working in batches, place the cooled mixture in the 40 oz. Processing Bowl with the yogurt and mint leaves. Pulse until smooth. Pour into a serving bowl and add the remaining broth. Stir well and chill before serving. Garnish with a dollop of crème fraiche. Serves 4.

CAL 269, FAT 16G, SAT FAT 8G, CHOL 44MG, SODIUM 605MG, CARBS 22G, PROTEIN 9G, FIBER 6G, CALCIUM 165MG, POTASSIUM 587MG

ROASTED GARLIC & ROMA TOMATO SOUP

2½ LBS. FRESH ROMA TOMATOES, SLICED IN HALF LENGTHWISE
1 MEDIUM YELLOW ONION, PEELED AND CUT INTO QUARTERS
8 CLOVES GARLIC, PEELED
3 TBSP. EXTRA VIRGIN OLIVE OIL
½ TSP. SALT
¼ TSP. GROUND BLACK PEPPER
1 CUP TOMATO JUICE
1 CUP HALF-AND-HALF CREAM
1 TBSP. FRESH BASIL LEAVES, CHOPPED
1 CUP HIGH-QUALITY CROUTONS FOR GARNISH

Preheat the oven to 375°F. Place the tomatoes, onion, and garlic in a single layer on a baking pan. Avoid over-crowding the vegetables. Drizzle with the olive oil and season with salt and pepper. Roast for 45 minutes, turning once or twice. Remove from the oven and let cool.

Working in batches, place the roasted vegetables in the 40 oz. Processing Bowl. Pulse each batch until smooth. Spoon into a large saucepan and add the tomato juice, cream and basil. Adjust the seasonings to taste. Warm over medium-low heat for about 5 minutes until barely simmering. Do not boil. Serve in 4 bowls with croutons to garnish. Serves 4.

CAL 286, FAT 20G, SAT FAT 7G, CHOL 24MG, SODIUM 513MG, CARBS 25G, PROTEIN 6G, FIBER 5G, CALCIUM 110MG, POTASSIUM 813MG

HEARTY VEGETABLE SOUP

1 MEDIUM YELLOW ONION, PEELED, ROUGHLY CUT
1 TBSP. EXTRA VIRGIN OLIVE OIL
2 CUPS KALE LEAVES
1 LB. BROCCOLI FLORETS
3 CUPS VEGETABLE BROTH
1 CARROT, PEELED AND SLICED
½ CUP CORN KERNELS (CANNED OR FROZEN)
1 CUP CANNED KIDNEY BEANS
1 CUP COOKED PASTA SHELLS
1 TSP. SALT
⅛ TSP. CAYENNE PEPPER
½ TSP. GROUND BLACK PEPPER
GRATED PARMESAN CHEESE FOR GARNISH

Place the onion in the Single Serve Cup and pulse until evenly chopped. Sauté the onion in the oil in a saucepot on medium heat until soft. Add the kale leaves, broccoli and vegetable broth. Bring to a boil; then reduce to a simmer. Cover and simmer for 5 minutes. Remove from heat and let cool.

Working in batches, place the cooled mixture in the 40 oz. Processing Bowl and pulse until smooth. Return to the saucepot. Add the carrots, corn, kidney beans and cooked pasta shells. Adjust the seasonings to taste and heat through on medium before serving. Garnish each serving with cheese. Makes 4 hearty servings.

CAL 213, FAT 6G, SAT FAT 2G, CHOL 5MG, SODIUM 1332MG,
CARBS 31G, PROTEIN 12G, FIBER 5G, CALCIUM 151MG, POTASSIUM 602MG

SMOKED HAM, SWEET POTATO & APPLE SOUP

4 LARGE SWEET POTATOES, BAKED AND COOLED, SKINS REMOVED
2 CUPS NATURAL APPLESAUCE, DIVIDED
2 CUPS REDUCED-SODIUM CHICKEN BROTH, DIVIDED
1 TSP. SALT (OR TO TASTE)
½ TSP. GROUND BLACK PEPPER
1 CUP SMOKED HAM, CUT INTO BITE-SIZED CUBES

Place one-third each of the sweet potatoes, applesauce and chicken broth in the 40 oz. Processing Bowl. Pulse each batch until smooth. Place the mixture in a large saucepot and bring the soup to a boil. Reduce to a simmer and season with salt and pepper to taste. Add the smoked ham and heat through again for a few minutes. Serves 4.

CAL 238, FAT 3G, SAT FAT 1G, CHOL 20MG, SODIUM 1525MG, CARBS 42G, PROTEIN 13G, FIBER 5G, CALCIUM 62MG, POTASSIUM 719MG

EAST INDIAN CURRIED CAULIFLOWER SOUP

½ SMALL ONION, PEELED, ROUGHLY CUT
1 TBSP. EXTRA VIRGIN OLIVE OIL
1 TSP. CURRY POWDER
¼ TSP. TURMERIC
¼ TSP. GROUND SWEET PAPRIKA
1 TSP. SALT
½ TSP. GROUND BLACK PEPPER
1 LB. CAULIFLOWER FLORETS
2 CUPS VEGETABLE BROTH

Place the onion in the Single Serve Cup and pulse until chopped. Cook the onion in the oil in a saucepot over medium-high heat until soft. Add the curry powder, turmeric, sweet paprika, salt, and pepper and cook for an additional minute. Add the cauliflower and broth and bring to a boil. Reduce to a simmer, cover, and let cook about 10 minutes. Remove from heat and let cool.

Working in batches, place cooled soup in the 40 oz. Processing Bowl and pulse until smooth. Season with additional salt and pepper as needed. Serve chilled or heat through and serve warm. Serves 3 to 4.

CAL 92, FAT 4G, SAT FAT 1G, CHOL 0MG, SODIUM 582MG,
CARBS 12G, PROTEIN 3G, FIBER 5G, CALCIUM 38MG, POTASSIUM 488MG

SPEEDY CHICKEN TORTILLA SOUP

1 MEDIUM YELLOW ONION, PEELED, QUARTERED
¼ TSP. CHILI POWDER
14 OZ. CAN FIRE-ROASTED TOMATOES, WITH JUICE
1 TBSP. FRESH CILANTRO LEAVES
2½ CUPS CHICKEN BROTH
1 CUP COOKED CHICKEN MEAT, SHREDDED
1 CUP COOKED KIDNEY BEANS (USE CANNED, IF DESIRED)
SALT AND PEPPER TO TASTE
DICED AVOCADO, SOUR CREAM, AND TORTILLA STRIPS (OPTIONAL)

Place the onion, chili powder, tomatoes with juice and cilantro in the 40 oz. Processing Bowl and pulse until smooth.

Pour the tomato mixture into a saucepot and add the broth, chicken and kidney beans, stirring well to combine. Add salt and pepper to taste. Heat on medium, stirring often, until the soup is simmering. Serve with garnishes of diced avocado, sour cream, and tortilla strips, if desired. Serves 4.

CAL 162, FAT 2G, SAT FAT 0G, CHOL 33MG, SODIUM 897MG,
CARBS 21G, PROTEIN 17G, FIBER 5G, CALCIUM 68MG, POTASSIUM 592MG

BABY SPINACH SALAD
WITH CHAMPAGNE HONEY VINAIGRETTE

6 CUPS BABY SPINACH LEAVES
8 CREMINI MUSHROOMS, SLICED AND SAUTÉED
¼ SMALL RED ONION, PEELED, ROUGHLY CUT
2 TBSP. CHAMPAGNE VINEGAR
2 TBSP. EXTRA VIRGIN OLIVE OIL
2 TBSP. RAW, UNFILTERED HONEY
1 TSP. SALT
½ TSP. GROUND BLACK PEPPER
4 TBSP. CRUMBLED FETA CHEESE, FOR GARNISH

In a large mixing bowl, combine the spinach leaves and mushrooms. Set aside.

Place the red onion in the Single Serve Cup and pulse until chopped. Add the onion to the spinach and mushrooms. Place the vinegar, oil, honey, salt and pepper in the Single Serve Cup and pulse to blend. Drizzle the vinaigrette over the salad to taste. Garnish each serving with a sprinkling of feta cheese. Serves 4 to 6.

CAL 138, FAT 9G, SAT FAT 3G, CHOL 9MG, SODIUM 724MG,
CARBS 9G, PROTEIN 4G, FIBER 1G, CALCIUM 95MG, POTASSIUM 408MG

CRISP BROCCOLI RABE & BLACK OLIVE TAPENADE SALAD

1 CLOVE GARLIC, PEELED
1 CUP BLACK OLIVES, PITTED
1 SMALL ROASTED RED PEPPER
1 TSP. EXTRA VIRGIN OLIVE OIL
1 TSP. SEA SALT
1 TSP. LEMON JUICE
2 TBSP. FLAT LEAF PARSLEY
1½ LBS. BROCCOLI RABE, STEAMED UNTIL CRISP, CHILLED
½ CUP PARMESAN CHEESE, GRATED

Place all ingredients, except the broccoli rabe and cheese, into the 40 oz. Processing Bowl and pulse, just until the olives are roughly chopped.

To assemble the salads, place the broccoli rabe equally on 4 plates and cover with a spoonful of the olive tapenade. Garnish each serving with the Parmesan cheese and serve right away. Serves 4.

CAL 245, FAT 16G, SAT FAT 3G, CHOL 11MG, SODIUM 1522MG,
CARBS 13G, PROTEIN 9G, FIBER 3G, CALCIUM 289MG, POTASSIUM 19MG

CHOPPED VEGETABLE SALAD
WITH DIJON VINAIGRETTE

1 CUP CANNED SLICED BEETS, DRAINED
2 GREEN ONIONS, CUT IN HALF
4 SMALL FRESH CARROTS, PEELED, ROUGHLY CUT
3 CUPS SMALL BROCCOLI FLORETS
2 TSP. DIJON MUSTARD
1 TBSP. FRESH LEMON JUICE
2 TBSP. EXTRA VIRGIN OLIVE OIL
½ TSP. SALT
½ TSP. GROUND BLACK PEPPER
⅛ TSP. CAYENNE PEPPER

Place the beets, onions and carrots in the 40 oz. Processing Bowl and pulse until largely chopped (do not over-mix). Spoon into a serving bowl and add the broccoli florets. Place the remaining ingredients in the Bowl and pulse until blended. Pour over the salad and toss well to combine. Serve right away or chill until serving. Serves 4.

CAL 146, FAT 7G, SAT FAT 1G, CHOL 0MG, SODIUM 557MG,
CARBS 19G, PROTEIN 3G, FIBER 5G, CALCIUM 56MG, POTASSIUM 470MG

SUPER GREEN SUNFLOWER SALAD

½ BUNCH DARK GREEN KALE, RIBS REMOVED, TORN INTO BITE-SIZED PIECES
1 BUNCH SWISS CHARD, RIBS REMOVED, TORN INTO BITE-SIZED PIECES
½ SMALL RED ONION, PEELED, ROUGHLY CUT
½ CARROT, PEELED, ROUGHLY CUT
½ CUP CANNED MANDARIN ORANGE SEGMENTS
1 TBSP. ORANGE JUICE
1 TBSP. RICE VINEGAR
1 TSP. SESAME OIL
1 TBSP. TAMARI (OR SOY SAUCE/LOW-SODIUM SOY SAUCE)
½ TSP. SUGAR
¼ CUP SALTED SUNFLOWER SEEDS

Place the kale and Swiss chard in a large serving bowl. Place the onion and carrots in the 40 oz. Processing Bowl and pulse to chop evenly. Spoon the vegetables over the greens and add the mandarin oranges.

Place the remaining ingredients, except the sunflower seeds, in the Bowl and pulse until blended. Pour over the salad, add the seeds, and toss well to combine. Chill before serving. Serves 4.

CAL 89, FAT 5G, SAT FAT 1G, CHOL 0MG, SODIUM 81MG,
CARBS 11G, PROTEIN 3G, FIBER 11G, CALCIUM 73MG, POTASSIUM 388MG

BOK CHOY SALAD
WITH CASHEW DRESSING

6 CUPS RAW BOK CHOY, CHOPPED
2 FRESH CARROTS, PEELED, ROUGHLY CUT
2 STALKS CELERY, ROUGHLY CUT
3 GREEN ONIONS, CUT IN HALF
½ CUP UNSALTED TOASTED CASHEWS, DIVIDED
1 TBSP. FRESH LEMON JUICE
1 TSP. TAMARI (OR SOY SAUCE/LOW SODIUM SOY SAUCE)
3 TBSP. FLAXSEED OIL
½ TSP. SALT
½ TSP. GROUND BLACK PEPPER

Spoon the bok choy into a serving bowl. Place the carrots, celery and green onions in the 40 oz. Processing Bowl and pulse until finely chopped and add the mixture to the bok choy.

Place one-fourth cup cashews, lemon juice, tamari, flaxseed oil, salt and black pepper in the Bowl and pulse until blended. Pour the dressing over the salad and toss well to combine. Garnish each serving with the remaining toasted cashews. Serves 4.

CAL 221, FAT 19G, SAT FAT 3G, CHOL 0MG, SODIUM 455MG, CARBS 11G, PROTEIN 5G, FIBER 2G, CALCIUM 130MG, POTASSIUM 200MG

ORANGE FENNEL SALAD

2 LARGE FENNEL BULBS, FRONDS DISCARDED, SLICED
2 FRESH ORANGES, PEELED, SEGMENTED
½ SMALL RED ONION, PEELED, QUARTERED
1 TBSP. FLAT LEAF PARSLEY
2 TBSP. FRESH ORANGE JUICE
1 TBSP. FRESH LEMON JUICE
3 TBSP. EXTRA VIRGIN OLIVE OIL
½ TSP. SALT
½ TSP. GROUND BLACK PEPPER

Place the fennel and orange segments in a large mixing bowl.

Place the onion, parsley, orange juice, lemon juice, olive oil, salt, and pepper in the Single Serve Cup and pulse until the onion is evenly chopped. Pour the dressing over the salad and toss well to combine. Serve right away or chill. Serves 4.

CAL 175, FAT 11G, SAT FAT 2G, CHOL 0MG, SODIUM 352MG, CARBS 21G, PROTEIN 2G, FIBER 6G, CALCIUM 91MG, POTASSIUM 672MG

MEXICAN CHICKEN SALAD
WITH CHIPOTLE LIME DRESSING

1 CUP COOKED CHICKEN, SHREDDED
1 CUP COOKED BLACK BEANS
1 CUP CORN KERNELS (FROZEN OR CANNED)
4 CUPS ROMAINE LETTUCE, SHREDDED
1 LARGE TOMATO, QUARTERED
1 TBSP. FRESH CILANTRO LEAVES
2 GREEN ONIONS, ROUGHLY CUT
1 CHIPOTLE PEPPER IN ADOBO SAUCE
½ CUP LOW FAT PLAIN YOGURT
1 TSP. FRESH LIME JUICE
½ TSP. SALT
¼ TSP. GROUND BLACK PEPPER

Place the chicken, black beans, corn and lettuce in a large serving bowl.

Place the tomato, cilantro and green onions in the Single Serve Cup and pulse once or twice to evenly chop. Add the tomato mixture to the chicken and lettuce.

Place the pepper, yogurt, lime juice, salt and pepper in the Single Serve Cup and pulse until smooth. Pour the dressing over the salad and toss lightly. Serve at once. Serves 4.

**CAL 189, FAT 2G, SAT FAT 1G, CHOL 32MG, SODIUM 583MG,
CARBS 25G, PROTEIN 17G, FIBER 6G, CALCIUM 57MG, POTASSIUM 376MG**

ASIAN SHRIMP SLAW
WITH GINGER SESAME VINAIGRETTE

6 CUPS NAPA (SAVOY) CABBAGE LEAVES, THINLY SLICED
1 LARGE RED BELL PEPPER, SEEDED, QUARTERED
1 TSP. FRESH GINGER
1 CUP SNOW PEAS, THINLY SLICED
2 CUPS COOKED LARGE SHRIMP, WITHOUT SHELLS
3 TBSP. RICE WINE VINEGAR
2 TSP. SESAME OIL
1 TSP. SOY SAUCE (OR LOW SODIUM SOY SAUCE)
2 TBSP. EXTRA VIRGIN OLIVE OIL
1 TBSP. TOASTED SESAME SEEDS
SALT AND PEPPER TO TASTE

Place the cabbage in a serving bowl. Place the red pepper and ginger in the Single Serve Cup and pulse to chop. Add to the cabbage. Add the snow peas and shrimp to the cabbage.

Place the rice wine vinegar, sesame oil, soy sauce and olive oil in the Single Serve Cup and pulse until blended. Pour the dressing over the salad and toss well to combine. Add salt and pepper to taste and serve right away. Top with the sesame seeds just before serving. Serves 4.

CAL 188, FAT 6G, SAT FAT 1G, CHOL 220MG, SODIUM 313MG, CARBS 9G, PROTEIN 27G, FIBER 3G, CALCIUM 125MG, POTASSIUM 558MG

BROCCOLI SALAD
WITH ALMOND MISO DRESSING

½ CUP SILKEN TOFU
3 TBSP. ALMOND BUTTER
2 TBSP. CANOLA OIL
2 TBSP. WATER
2 TBSP. APPLE CIDER VINEGAR
2 TBSP. SWEET WHITE MISO
2 TBSP. GREEN ONION, CHOPPED
2 TSP. SUGAR
1 TBSP. FRESH PARSLEY
2 TSP. TAMARI (OR SOY SAUCE/LOW SODIUM SOY SAUCE)
2 HEADS BROCCOLI, CUT IN FLORETS, STEAMED AND CHILLED

Combine all ingredients, except the broccoli, in the Single Serve Cup and pulse until smooth. Pour the dressing over the broccoli to taste and toss well to combine. Serve right away. Serves 4. *(Cook's note: refrigerate remaining dressing in a tightly-covered container for up to 2 days.)*

CAL 256, FAT 17G, SAT FAT 2G, CHOL 0MG, SODIUM 610MG,
CARBS 22G, PROTEIN 11G, FIBER 6G, CALCIUM 156MG, POTASSIUM 793MG

CHICKEN CAESAR SALAD

2 BONELESS, SKINLESS CHICKEN BREASTS, GRILLED AND SLICED
6 CUPS ROMAINE LETTUCE, TORN
½ CUP SILKEN TOFU
¼ CUP BUTTERMILK
2 TBSP. FRESH LEMON JUICE
1 TBSP. WHITE WINE VINEGAR
2 TSP. DIJON MUSTARD
1 CLOVE GARLIC, PEELED
2 CANNED ANCHOVIES
1 CUP SEASONED SALAD CROUTONS
¼ CUP PARMESAN CHEESE, SHAVED

In a large mixing bowl, combine the chicken slices and the lettuce. Set aside.

In the Single Serve Cup, place the tofu, buttermilk, lemon juice, vinegar, mustard, garlic and anchovies. Pulse until creamy. Pour the dressing over the salad to taste and toss to coat. Add the croutons and Parmesan cheese just prior to serving. Serves 4 to 5.

CAL 190, FAT 7G, SAT FAT 1G, CHOL 37MG, SODIUM 398MG,
CARBS 16G, PROTEIN 16G, FIBER 2G, CALCIUM 105MG, POTASSIUM 282MG

APPLE, RED ONION & CRANBERRY SALAD WITH ALMOND VINAIGRETTE

6 CUPS BABY SPINACH LEAVES
1 LARGE RIPE GALA APPLE, PEELED, CORED AND SLICED
½ SMALL RED ONION, PEELED, THINLY SLICED
½ CUP DRIED CRANBERRIES
¼ CUP CRUMBLED GOAT CHEESE
3 TBSP. SHERRY VINEGAR
¼ CUP ALMOND OIL
½ TSP. DIJON MUSTARD
¼ TSP. SALT
¼ TSP. GROUND BLACK PEPPER
¼ CUP TOASTED, SLICED ALMONDS

In a large mixing bowl, combine the spinach, apple, onion, cranberries and cheese.

Combine the vinegar, oil, mustard, salt and pepper in the Single Serve Cup and pulse until blended. Toss the salad with the vinaigrette and top with the sliced almonds. Serves 4.

CAL 384, FAT 20G, SAT FAT 4G, CHOL 11MG, SODIUM 257MG,
CARBS 25G, PROTEIN 7G, FIBER 5G, CALCIUM 119MG, POTASSIUM 438MG

THREE BEAN SALAD WITH ITALIAN HERB VINAIGRETTE

2 STALKS CELERY, QUARTERED
½ SMALL RED ONION, PEELED, ROUGHLY CUT
½ CUP FLAT-LEAF PARSLEY
1 TBSP. FRESH BASIL
¾ LB. TRIMMED GREEN BEANS, CUT INTO 1-INCH PIECES, STEAMED AND COOLED
14 OZ. CAN OF GARBANZO BEANS, DRAINED
14 OZ. CAN OF RED KIDNEY BEANS, DRAINED
2 TBSP. EXTRA VIRGIN OLIVE OIL
2 TBSP. RED WINE VINEGAR
1 TBSP. LEMON JUICE
2 TSP. DIJON MUSTARD
1 TSP. SALT
½ TSP. GROUND BLACK PEPPER

Place the celery, onion, parsley and basil in the 40 oz. Processing Bowl and pulse until chopped evenly.

Spoon the mixture into a large serving bowl and add the beans.

Place the oil, vinegar, juice, mustard, salt and pepper in the Single Serve Cup. Pulse to blend and pour over the salad to taste. Toss well. Chill for at least 1 hour or up to overnight before serving. Serves 6.

CAL 177, FAT 6G, SAT FAT 0G, CHOL 0MG, SODIUM 730MG,
CARBS 27G, PROTEIN 7G, FIBER 7G, CALCIUM 63MG, POTASSIUM 383MG

ARUGULA, NECTARINE & PECAN SALAD WITH BLUE CHEESE DRESSING

6-8 CUPS ARUGULA LEAVES
2 RIPE NECTARINES, PITTED
2 TBSP. EXTRA VIRGIN OLIVE OIL
2 TBSP. FRESH LEMON JUICE
1 TBSP. RAW, UNFILTERED HONEY
1 TBSP. SHALLOT, PEELED, ROUGHLY CUT (OR USE SWEET WHITE ONION)
½ TSP. SALT
¼ TSP. GROUND BLACK PEPPER
⅓ CUP CRUMBLED BLUE CHEESE
⅓ CUP TOASTED PECANS

Place the arugula on 4 individual salad plates. Set aside. Place the nectarines in the 40 oz. Processing Bowl and pulse briefly to chop. Spoon the nectarines equally over the arugula.

Place the olive oil, lemon juice, honey, shallot, salt and pepper in the Bowl and pulse until smooth. Drizzle the dressing over each of the salads and top each salad with the blue cheese and toasted pecans. Serves 4.

CAL 255, FAT 20G, SAT FAT 5G, CHOL 8MG, SODIUM 454MG, CARBS 15G, PROTEIN 5G, FIBER 3G, CALCIUM 122MG, POTASSIUM 345MG

WHEATBERRY SALAD
WITH WALNUT SHALLOT VINAIGRETTE

½ SMALL RED ONION, PEELED, QUARTERED
½ CUP FLAT-LEAF PARSELY
½ SMALL RED BELL PEPPER, SEEDED, QUARTERED
2 CUPS COOKED WHEATBERRIES, COOLED
3 TBSP. SHERRY VINEGAR
2 TBSP. WALNUT OIL
1 MEDIUM SHALLOT, PEELED (OR USE SWEET WHITE ONION)
1 TSP. DIJON MUSTARD
½ TSP. SALT
¼ TSP. GROUND BLACK PEPPER
½ CUP WALNUTS, SHELLED

Place the onion, parsley and red pepper in the Single Serve Cup and pulse until chopped. Spoon the mixture into a large serving bowl and add the wheatberries. Mix to combine. Set aside.

Place the vinegar, oil, shallot, mustard, salt and pepper in the Single Serve Cup and pulse until blended. Pour the dressing over the salad and toss well. Chill at least 1 hour before serving. Just before serving, place the walnuts in the Single Serve Cup and pulse to chop. Mix the chopped walnuts into the salad and serve. Serves 3 to 4.

CAL 251, FAT 10G, SAT FAT 1G, CHOL 0MG, SODIUM 592MG,
CARBS 35G, PROTEIN 7G, FIBER 0G, CALCIUM 13MG, POTASSIUM 109MG

BRUSSELS SPROUT SALAD
WITH MAPLE-MUSTARD DRESSING

2 CUPS WHOLE BRUSSELS SPROUTS, SLICED THINLY
1 CUP CAULIFLOWER FLORETS, SLICED THINLY
6 OZ. CAN MANDARIN ORANGES, DRAINED
½ SMALL RED ONION, PEELED, ROUGHLY CUT
1 TBSP. DARK SESAME OIL
1 TBSP. RICE WINE VINEGAR
2 TSP. PURE MAPLE SYRUP
2 TSP. DIJON MUSTARD
¼ CUP DRIED CRANBERRIES

Place the sprouts, cauliflower and mandarin oranges in a large serving bowl. Set aside. Place the red onion in the Single Serve Cup and pulse until chopped. Add the onion to the salad.

Place the sesame oil, vinegar, syrup and mustard in the Single Serve Cup and pulse to blend. Pour over the salad and add the cranberries. Toss well and serve at once. Serves 4.

CAL 100, FAT 4G, SAT FAT 1G, CHOL 0MG, SODIUM 24MG,
CARBS 17G, PROTEIN 3G, FIBER 4G, CALCIUM 36MG, POTASSIUM 319MG

ALBACORE TUNA & DILL SALAD

2 STALKS CELERY, QUARTERED
¼ MEDIUM RED ONION, PEELED
4 SPEARS DILL PICKLE
3-6 OZ. CANS OF ALBACORE TUNA IN WATER, DRAINED AND CHUNKED
½ CUP LOW FAT GREEK YOGURT
3 TBSP. MAYONNAISE
1 TBSP. FRESH DILL
2 TSP. DIJON MUSTARD
1 TSP. SALT
½ TSP. GROUND BLACK PEPPER
1 TBSP. CREAM (OR USE LOW FAT MILK), PLUS MORE TO TASTE
8 CUPS SALAD GREENS, RINSED AND KEPT CRISP
WHOLE GRAIN CRACKERS

Place the celery, onion and pickle in the 40 oz. Processing Bowl and pulse to chop. Spoon the mixture into a large mixing bowl and add the tuna.

Place the yogurt, mayonnaise, dill, mustard, salt and pepper in the Single Serve Cup and pulse until smooth. Add cream as needed to taste. Pour the dressing over the tuna salad and mix well to coat. Serve on a bed of salad greens with whole grain crackers on the side. Serves 6 to 8.

CAL 85, FAT 3G, SAT FAT 0G, CHOL 13MG, SODIUM 461MG, CARBS 5G, PROTEIN 7G, FIBER 8G, CALCIUM 39MG, POTASSIUM 183MG

OLD EL PASO CHICKEN WITH TOASTED PUMPKIN MOLE SAUCE – P. 153
GUSTIAMO'S GRILLED PESTO CHICKEN – P. 154
NEW ORLEANS CHICKEN & SHRIMP JAMBALAYA – P. 155
SESAME CHICKEN LO MEIN – P. 156
CHICKEN & JACK CHEESE ENCHILADAS – P. 157
GREEK CHICKEN WITH FETA & OLIVE STUFFING – P. 158
EASY TOMATO & BASIL CREAM SAUCE – P. 159
GRILLED SALMON WITH MAPLE DIJON SAUCE – P. 160
ROASTED SALMON WITH YOGURT DILL SAUCE – P. 161
JAPANESE HALIBUT WITH MISO-LIME GLAZE – P. 162
GRILLED TILAPIA WITH ROMESCO SAUCE – P. 163

CHAPTER SIX :: ENTRÉES & SIDE DISHES

BAJA FISH TACOS – P. 164
GRILLED LAMB SKEWERS WITH LEMON-GARLIC MINT SAUCE – P. 165
CRANBERRY-MUSTARD ROASTED PORK LOIN – P. 166
BEEF FLANK STEAK WITH CHIMICHURRI SAUCE – P. 167
CORNISH BEEF PASTIES – P. 168
CHICKEN & GARDEN VEGGIE PASTIES – P. 169
TENDER-CRISP BROCCOLI WITH FRESH HERB SAUCE – P. 170
SUPER SNAP PEAS WITH TAHINI MISO SAUCE – P. 171
PARMESAN CAULIFLOWER CUPS – P. 172
SPRINGTIME PEA PUREE – P. 173
TENDER-CRISP ASPARAGUS WITH HOLLANDAISE SAUCE – P. 174
TOMATOES GREMOLATA – P. 175

BAJA FISH TACOS – P. 164

CHICKEN & JACK CHEESE ENCHILADAS – P. 157

TOMATOES GREMOLATA – P. 175

NEW ORLEANS CHICKEN & SHRIMP JAMBALAYA – P. 155

OLD EL PASO CHICKEN
WITH TOASTED PUMPKIN MOLE SAUCE

1 CUP HULLED PUMPKIN SEEDS, TOASTED
1 SMALL WHITE ONION, ROUGHLY CUT
3 CLOVES GARLIC, PEELED
¼ CUP FRESH CILANTRO LEAVES, PLUS MORE FOR GARNISH
2 ROMAINE LETTUCE LEAVES, ROUGHLY TORN
½ SERRANO PEPPER, SEEDED
½ TSP. GROUND CUMIN
2½ CUPS CHICKEN OR VEGETABLE BROTH, PLUS 1 CUP AS NEEDED
1 TBSP. CANOLA OIL
1 TSP. SALT
4 SMALL BONELESS, SKINLESS CHICKEN BREASTS
4 TO 6 CUPS BROWN RICE, STEAMED AND KEPT WARM
CILANTRO FOR GARNISH, OPTIONAL

Place the pumpkin seeds, onion, garlic, cilantro, lettuce, pepper and cumin in the 40 oz. Processing Bowl. Add ½ cup broth and pulse until smooth. Add ½ cup broth and pulse again briefly. In a large skillet, heat the oil on medium-high heat. Add the blender mixture to the skillet and cook until very thick. Whisk in the remaining 1½ cups of chicken broth and add the salt and chicken. Add up to 1 cup additional broth, if desired. Bring to a boil and reduce to a simmer; cook for 8 minutes or until chicken is cooked through and no pink remains. To serve, divide the rice between 4 dinner plates and top with the chicken and sauce. Garnish with cilantro, if desired. Serves 4.

CAL 526, FAT 12G, SAT FAT 3G, CHOL 96MG, SODIUM 947MG, CARBS 57G, PROTEIN 45G, FIBER 4G, CALCIUM 63MG, POTASSIUM 687MG

GUSTIAMO'S GRILLED PESTO CHICKEN

1 CUP FRESH BASIL LEAVES
2 TBSP. EXTRA VIRGIN OLIVE OIL
¼ CUP TOASTED PINE NUTS
¼ CUP PARMESAN CHEESE, GRATED
2 TBSP. WATER
1 CLOVE GARLIC, PEELED
½ LEMON, JUICED
½ TSP. SALT
½ TSP. GROUND BLACK PEPPER
4 SMALL BONELESS, SKINLESS CHICKEN BREASTS, GRILLED OR BROILED

Place the basil, olive oil, pine nuts, cheese, water, garlic, lemon, salt and pepper in the 40 oz. Processing Bowl. Pulse until smooth. To serve, place the cooked chicken breasts on 4 dinner plates and spoon the pesto sauce equally over each serving. Serves 4.

CAL 374, FAT 22G, SAT FAT 1G, CHOL 99MG, SODIUM 470MG,
CARBS 2G, PROTEIN 38G, FIBER 2G, CALCIUM 50MG, POTASSIUM 294MG

NEW ORLEANS CHICKEN & SHRIMP JAMBALAYA

2 CLOVES GARLIC, PEELED
1 SMALL WHITE ONION, PEELED AND ROUGHLY CUT
½ CUP GREEN BELL PEPPER, SEEDED AND ROUGHLY CUT
1 CUP CANNED FIRE-ROASTED DICED TOMATOES, WITH JUICES
1 TSP. CAJUN SEASONING
½ TSP. TABASCO® SAUCE
2 CUPS CHICKEN BROTH
1 CUP LONG GRAIN WHITE RICE (OR QUICK-COOKING BROWN RICE)
½ LB. COOKED CHICKEN THIGH MEAT, CUT INTO BITE-SIZED PIECES
½ LB. MEDIUM SHRIMP, PEELED, DEVEINED
SALT AND PEPPER TO TASTE

Place the garlic, onion, green pepper, tomatoes, seasoning and Tabasco® sauce in the 40 oz. Processing Bowl and pulse just until chopped. Spoon into a large sauté pan and add the broth and rice. Bring to a boil on high heat; cover and reduce to a simmer for 20 minutes. Add the chicken and shrimp and cook for about 5 minutes until the shrimp are cooked through. Adjust seasonings to taste before serving. Serves 4.

CAL 320, FAT 11G, SAT FAT 3G, CHOL 81MG, SODIUM 567MG,
CARBS 30G, PROTEIN 11G, FIBER 4G, CALCIUM 67MG, POTASSIUM 549MG

SESAME CHICKEN LO MEIN

1 CLOVE GARLIC, CHOPPED
½ SMALL WHITE ONION, CHOPPED
2 TBSP. CANOLA OIL, DIVIDED
1 RED BELL PEPPER, SEEDED, CUT IN STRIPS
4 SMALL BONELESS, SKINLESS CHICKEN BREASTS, CUT IN STRIPS
1 TSP. SESAME OIL
¼ CUP TAMARI (OR USE LOW SODIUM SOY SAUCE)
2 TBSP. CREAMY PEANUT BUTTER
¼ TSP. GROUND BLACK PEPPER
½ LB. SPAGHETTI NOODLES, COOKED, KEPT WARM
2 TBSP. FRESH CILANTRO LEAVES, CHOPPED
2 TBSP. PEANUTS, CHOPPED

Sauté the garlic and onion in the canola oil over medium-high heat. Add the red pepper and chicken and reduce the heat to medium. Sauté for about 5 minutes, or until the chicken is no longer pink.

Meanwhile, pulse the sesame oil, tamari, peanut butter and black pepper in the Single Serve Cup until smooth. Stir into the chicken and peppers and heat through.

To serve, toss the chicken and peppers with the noodles and garnish with the cilantro and peanuts before serving. Serves 4.

CAL 511, FAT 23G, SAT FAT 4G, CHOL 96MG, SODIUM 785MG, CARBS 30G, PROTEIN 40G, FIBER 3G, CALCIUM 30MG, POTASSIUM 428MG

CHICKEN & JACK CHEESE ENCHILADAS

1 JALAPEÑO PEPPER, SEEDED AND ROASTED
28 OZ. CANNED WHOLE TOMATOES WITH JUICES
1 MEDIUM ONION, PEELED, ROUGHLY CUT
1 TBSP. CANOLA OIL, PLUS MORE FOR TORTILLAS
2 CUPS REDUCED-SODIUM CHICKEN BROTH
1 TSP. SALT
2 CUPS COOKED CHICKEN, SHREDDED
12 CORN TORTILLAS, WARMED
⅔ CUP MONTEREY JACK CHEESE, SHREDDED

Place the pepper, tomatoes and onion in the 40 oz. Processing Bowl and pulse until evenly chopped. Heat the oil in a large saucepan and add the chopped vegetables. Sauté until slightly thickened; add the chicken broth and salt. Reduce the heat and simmer the sauce for 10 minutes.

Preheat the oven to 350°F. Spread one-half cup of the sauce in a 9 x 13-inch baking dish. Roll up a portion of the chicken in each tortilla, and place in the casserole dish, seam side down. Pour the remaining tomato sauce over the dish and top with the cheese. Bake until the enchiladas are heated through and the cheese is melted, about 20 minutes. Serves 4 to 6.

CAL 275, FAT 10G, SAT FAT 5G, CHOL 40MG, SODIUM 743MG,
CARBS 29G, PROTEIN 18G, FIBER 5G, CALCIUM 221MG, POTASSIUM 478MG

GREEK CHICKEN WITH FETA & OLIVE STUFFING

¾ CUP GREEK FETA CHEESE, CRUMBLED
10 OZ. PKG. FROZEN SPINACH, THAWED AND SQUEEZED DRY
8 KALAMATA OLIVES, PITTED
1 TBSP. EXTRA VIRGIN OLIVE OIL
1 TBSP. FRESH LEMON JUICE
4 BONELESS, SKINLESS CHICKEN BREASTS, SEASONED WITH SALT AND PEPPER

Preheat oven to 400°F. Place the cheese, spinach, olives, oil and lemon juice in the 40 oz. Processing Bowl. Pulse until the ingredients are mixed together and coarsely chopped. Set aside.

Make a horizontal slit in each chicken breast through the thickest part. Pack the stuffing into each breast, dividing the filling evenly. Use cooking string or a toothpick to secure the pocket, if needed.

Lightly coat a rimmed baking sheet with cooking spray and place the chicken breasts on the sheet. Bake for 8 minutes. Turn the chicken over and bake for another 8 minutes, or until cooked through and no pink remains. Remove string or toothpicks before serving. Serves 4.

CAL 326, FAT 15G, SAT FAT 6G, CHOL 121MG, SODIUM 655MG,
CARBS 4G, PROTEIN 41G, FIBER 1G, CALCIUM 198MG, POTASSIUM 307MG

EASY TOMATO & BASIL CREAM SAUCE

1 RIPE ROMA TOMATO, SEEDED AND QUARTERED
2 TBSP. TOMATO PASTE
⅓ CUP HEAVY CREAM
6 BASIL LEAVES
¼ TSP. DRIED ITALIAN SEASONING

Place all ingredients in the Single Serve Cup and pulse until smooth. Heat the sauce over medium heat in a small saucepan or heat briefly in the microwave.

Serve over hot, cooked pasta or add vegetables and/or cooked meat to create a complete entrée. Makes about ¾ cup sauce.

CAL 81, FAT 8G, SAT FAT 5G, CHOL 27MG, SODIUM 35MG,
CARBS 4G, PROTEIN 1G, FIBER 1G, CALCIUM 16MG, POTASSIUM 163MG

GRILLED SALMON
WITH MAPLE DIJON SAUCE

2 TBSP. EXTRA VIRGIN OLIVE OIL
2 TBSP. DIJON MUSTARD
1 TBSP. PURE MAPLE SYRUP
1 TBSP. FRESH PARSLEY LEAVES
1 CLOVE GARLIC, PEELED
½ TSP. SALT
¼ TSP. GROUND BLACK PEPPER
4 8 OZ. SALMON FILLETS, WITH SKIN

Preheat a grill to medium-high heat. In the Single Serve Cup, place the olive oil, mustard, syrup, parsley, garlic, salt and pepper. Pulse until smooth. Set aside one-half of the Dijon sauce. Brush the remaining half over the salmon fillets.

Grill the salmon over medium-high heat, 4 to 5 minutes on each side. Remove from grill and let rest for 5 minutes. Brush with the remaining sauce. Serves 4.

CAL 463, FAT 27G, SAT FAT 2G, CHOL 139MG, SODIUM 481MG,
CARBS 4G, PROTEIN 48G, FIBER 0G, CALCIUM 36MG, POTASSIUM 22MG

ROASTED SALMON
WITH YOGURT DILL SAUCE

4 6 OZ. SALMON FILLETS, SEASONED WITH SALT, PEPPER AND BRUSHED WITH OLIVE OIL
1 CUP LOW FAT PLAIN GREEK YOGURT
1 TBSP. FRESH DILL
1 TBSP. FRESH LEMON JUICE
1 CLOVE GARLIC, PEELED
1 TSP. SALT
½ TSP. GROUND BLACK PEPPER

Preheat oven to 450°F degrees.

Lightly coat a baking dish with cooking spray and position the fillets in the dish. Roast in the oven for 10 minutes, until just cooked through.

Meanwhile, place the yogurt, dill, lemon juice, garlic, salt, and pepper in the Single Serve Cup and pulse until smooth. Serve each salmon fillet with a dollop of the dill sauce. Serves 4.

CAL 333, FAT 4G, SAT FAT 1G, CHOL 108MG, SODIUM 685MG,
CARBS 2G, PROTEIN 42G, FIBER 0G, CALCIUM 67MG, POTASSIUM 581MG

JAPANESE HALIBUT WITH MISO-LIME GLAZE

2 TBSP. WHITE MISO PASTE
2 TBSP. MIRIN OR SWEET WHITE WINE
1 TBSP. SOY SAUCE OR TAMARI (OR USE LOW SODIUM SOY SAUCE)
1 TSP. FRESH GINGER
1 TBSP. FRESH LIME JUICE
4 6 OZ. HALIBUT FILLETS (OR USE OTHER MILD, WHITE FISH FILLETS)
1 TBSP. TOASTED SESAME SEEDS

Preheat oven to 450°F.

Place the miso, mirin, soy sauce, ginger and lime juice in the Single Serve Cup and pulse until smooth. Brush the miso glaze mixture all over the halibut fillets.

Line a baking tray with foil and coat with cooking spray. Place the halibut on the tray and roast for 10 minutes, until just cooked through. Let rest 5 minutes and sprinkle with toasted sesame seeds. Serves 4.

CAL 254, FAT 8G, SAT FAT 1G, CHOL55MG, SODIUM 693MG,
CARBS 5G, PROTEIN 39G, FIBER 1G, CALCIUM 157MG, POTASSIUM 55MG

GRILLED TILAPIA WITH ROMESCO SAUCE

¼ CUP EXTRA VIRGIN OLIVE OIL
1 SLICE CRUSTY BREAD, TORN AND TOASTED
½ CUP BLANCHED, PEELED ALMONDS, TOASTED
5 CLOVES GARLIC, PEELED
15 OZ. CANNED WHOLE TOMATOES WITH JUICE
4 OZ. JARRED ROASTED RED BELL PEPPERS, DRAINED
1 TBSP. GROUND SMOKED PAPRIKA
2 TBSP. RED WINE VINEGAR
4 6 OZ. TILAPIA FILLETS, SEASONED WITH SALT AND PEPPER AND BRUSHED WITH OLIVE OIL (OR USE OTHER MILD, WHITE FISH FILLETS)

Preheat oven to 350°F. Cover a rimmed baking sheet with foil. Set aside. Place the olive oil, bread, almonds, garlic, tomatoes, bell peppers, paprika and vinegar in the 40 oz. Processing Bowl. Blend until smooth. Spread the mixture over the foil-covered baking sheet and bake in the oven for 15 minutes until the edges caramelize. Remove from heat and let cool.

Heat a grill to medium high heat. Grill the fish, 4-5 minutes per side. Remove and let rest for 5 minutes. Serve with the Romesco sauce drizzled on top. Serves 4.

CAL 414, FAT 26G, SAT FAT 4G, CHOL 65MG, SODIUM 229MG, CARBS 13G, PROTEIN 36G, FIBER 0G, CALCIUM 103MG, POTASSIUM 927MG

BAJA FISH TACOS

½ CUP FRESH CILANTRO LEAVES
1 LIME, JUICED
1 TBSP. RAW, UNFILTERED HONEY
½ CUP LOW FAT MAYONNAISE
¼ RED CABBAGE, THINLY SLICED
SALT AND BLACK PEPPER TO TASTE
3 TBSP. CANOLA OIL
12 SMALL FRESH CORN TORTILLAS
1 LB. WHITE FISH FILLETS, CUT INTO BITE-SIZED PIECES
1 AVOCADO, CHOPPED
½ CUP FRESH PREPARED SALSA

Place the cilantro, lime juice, honey and mayonnaise in the 40 oz. Processing Bowl and pulse until smooth. Place the cabbage in a large mixing bowl and spoon the dressing over, tossing lightly to mix. Season with the salt and pepper to taste. Chill.

In a large sauté pan, heat the oil until shimmering. Using tongs, quickly dip the tortillas into the oil just until the tortillas are softened. Drain the tortillas on paper towels. Remove all but 1 tablespoon of oil from the pan and heat on medium. Add the fish and sauté, stirring often, until slightly crispy and cooked through. Set aside and keep warm.

To assemble, place a spoonful of the cabbage slaw in one tortilla, top with a few pieces of fish and add the avocado and salsa. Repeat with the remaining tacos. Serve right away. Serves 4 to 6.

CAL 364, FAT 12G, SAT FAT 1G, CHOL 50MG, SODIUM 383MG, CARBS 43G, PROTEIN 24G, FIBER 8G, CALCIUM 64MG, POTASSIUM 379MG

GRILLED LAMB SKEWERS
WITH LEMON-GARLIC MINT SAUCE

4 CLOVES GARLIC, PEELED
2 TBSP. FRESH LEMON JUICE
¼ CUP EXTRA VIRGIN OLIVE OIL
½ CUP FRESH MINT LEAVES
1½ LBS. TOP ROUND LAMB, CUT INTO 1-INCH CUBES
1 LARGE RED ONION, CUT INTO 1-INCH SECTIONS
1 PINT CHERRY TOMATOES
1 TSP. SALT
½ TSP. GROUND BLACK PEPPER
WOODEN SKEWERS, SOAKED IN WATER

In the Single Serve Cup, place the garlic, lemon juice, olive oil and mint. Pulse until smooth. Reserve half of the mint sauce. Place the remaining half of the sauce in a medium mixing bowl with the lamb cubes. Cover and let marinate for 1 hour (or up to 8 hours).

Thread 3 to 4 lamb cubes on each wooden skewer, alternating with the red onion and cherry tomatoes. Season with the salt and pepper. Heat a grill to medium-high and grill the lamb skewers to medium-rare or medium for the lamb (about 6 to 10 minutes), turning 2-3 times. Place cooked skewers on a platter and drizzle with the reserved mint sauce. Serves 4.

CAL 377, FAT 10G, SAT FAT 6G, CHOL 107MG, SODIUM 676MG, CARBS 5G, PROTEIN 34G, FIBER 0G, CALCIUM 22MG, POTASSIUM 425MG

CRANBERRY-MUSTARD ROASTED PORK LOIN

14 OZ. CANNED WHOLE CRANBERRY SAUCE
3 TBSP. DIJON MUSTARD
1 SHALLOT, PEELED, ROUGHLY CUT (OR USE ¼ SMALL WHITE ONION)
1 TBSP. RED WINE VINEGAR
1 TBSP. RAW, UNFILTERED HONEY
1 TBSP. FRESH ROSEMARY LEAVES
2½ LBS. BONELESS PORK LOIN
SALT AND PEPPER TO TASTE

Preheat oven to 475°F. Place the cranberry sauce, mustard, shallot, vinegar, honey, and rosemary in the 40 oz. Processing Bowl. Pulse until smooth. Reserve half of the sauce.

Place the pork loin in a heavy roasting pan. Season with salt and pepper. Cover the loin with half of the sauce. Place in the oven and roast for 30-40 minutes, until internal temperature has reached 140°F. Remove from the oven and let rest 15 minutes. Serve with the reserved half of the cranberry sauce. Serves 6.

CAL 350, FAT 11G, SAT FAT 4G, CHOL 92MG, SODIUM 101MG,
CARBS 28G, PROTEIN 32G, FIBER 1G, CALCIUM 20MG, POTASSIUM 480MG

BEEF FLANK STEAK
WITH CHIMICHURRI SAUCE

1½ LB. BEEF FLANK STEAK
SALT AND PEPPER FOR SEASONING
1 CUP FRESH ITALIAN PARSLEY, PACKED
½ CUP EXTRA VIRGIN OLIVE OIL
⅓ CUP RED WINE VINEGAR
¼ CUP FRESH CILANTRO, PACKED
2 CLOVES GARLIC, PEELED
¾ TSP. DRIED CRUSHED RED PEPPER
½ TSP. GROUND CUMIN
½ TSP. SALT

Preheat the oven to 450°F. Place the steak in a roasting pan and season with salt and pepper. Roast for 15 minutes, reduce the heat to 350°F and roast for another 15 to 20 minutes, until the internal temperature of the meat reaches 125°F. Remove from the oven and let rest for 15 minutes. Slice thinly across the grain and keep warm.

Meanwhile, in the 40 oz. Processing Bowl, pulse the remaining ingredients until smooth. To serve, fan the steak slices on a serving platter and drizzle with the Chimichurri Sauce. Serves 6.

CAL 188, FAT 16G, SAT FAT 5G, CHOL 60MG, SODIUM 231MG,
CARBS 2G, PROTEIN 23G, FIBER 0G, CALCIUM 11MG, POTASSIUM 42MG

CORNISH BEEF PASTIES

½ PÂTE BRISÉE (SEE P. 183)
4 SMALL POTATOES, PEELED, THINLY SLICED
½ WHITE ONION, PEELED, ROUGHLY CUT
2 TBSP. FLAT LEAF PARSLEY
½ LB. BEEF SIRLOIN STEAK, CUT IN LARGE PIECES
¼ CUP BUTTER
SALT AND PEPPER TO TASTE

Preheat the oven to 450°F. Divide the dough into quarters and roll each into a 7-inch circle. Place equal amounts of the potatoes in the center of each pastry circle.

Place the onion, parsley and beef in the 40 oz. Processing Bowl and pulse until just chopped. Do not over-mix. Layer equally on top of the potatoes. Dot each pasty with the butter and generously salt and pepper to taste. To assemble, bring the edges of the pasty together, tucking in the ends, and crimp in a fluted pattern. Lightly pierce the pastry with a fork to allow the steam to escape. Place the pasties on a baking sheet and bake for 15 minutes. Reduce the heat to 350°F and continue baking for 30 minutes. Serve while warm. Serves 4.

CAL 435, FAT 13G, SAT FAT 7G, CHOL 11MG, SODIUM 587MG,
CARBS 26G, PROTEIN 25G, FIBER 3G, CALCIUM 5MG, POTASSIUM 308MG

CHICKEN & GARDEN VEGGIE PASTIES

½ PÂTE BRISÉE (SEE P. 183)
4 SMALL POTATOES, PEELED, THINLY SLICED
½ WHITE ONION, PEELED, ROUGHLY CUT
1 LARGE CARROT, PEELED, CUT IN QUARTERS
¾ CUP PETITE PEAS, FRESH OR FROZEN, THAWED
2 CUPS CHICKEN BREAST MEAT, COOKED, SHREDDED
1 TBSP. FLAT-LEAF PARSLEY, CHOPPED
SALT AND PEPPER TO TASTE

Preheat the oven to 450°F. Divide the dough into quarters and roll each into a 7-inch circle. Place equal amounts of the potatoes in the center of each pastry circle.

Place the onion and carrot into the 40 oz. Processing Bowl and pulse to chop. Remove and spoon on top of the potatoes. Layer the peas and chicken on each pasty. Scatter the parsley, salt and pepper over all. To assemble, bring the edges of the pasty together, tucking in the ends, and crimp in a fluted pattern. Lightly pierce the pastry with a fork to allow the steam to escape. Place the pasties on a baking sheet and bake for 15 minutes. Reduce the heat to 350°F and continue baking for 15 minutes. Serve while warm. Serves 4.

CAL 346, FAT 12G, SAT FAT 3G, CHOL 68MG, SODIUM 683MG,
CARBS 21G, PROTEIN 27G, FIBER 3G, CALCIUM 44MG, POTASSIUM 569MG

TENDER-CRISP BROCCOLI WITH FRESH HERB SAUCE

1 LB. BROCCOLI FLORETS, STEAMED AND BLANCHED, WARM
1 CUP WATERCRESS LEAVES, TIGHTLY PACKED
1 CUP LOW FAT PLAIN YOGURT
¼ CUP LOW FAT MAYONNAISE
2 TBSP. FRESH DILL
2 TBSP. FRESH BASIL LEAVES
2 TBSP. FRESH MINT LEAVES
1 GREEN ONION, ROUGHLY CUT
1 TSP. RED WINE VINEGAR
½ TSP. SALT

Place the broccoli florets in a serving bowl.

Place the remaining ingredients in the 40 oz. Processing Bowl and pulse until smooth. Pour over the broccoli florets and toss to coat. Serve while warm or chill before serving. Serves 4.

CAL 72, FAT 2G, SAT FAT 1G, CHOL 4MG, SODIUM 479MG,
CARBS 9G, PROTEIN 3G, FIBER 0G, CALCIUM 116MG, POTASSIUM 155MG

SUGAR SNAP PEAS
WITH TAHINI MISO SAUCE

1 LB. SUGAR SNAP PEAS, TRIMMED, STEAMED FOR 2 MINUTES AND BLANCHED
¼ CUP WATER
1 TBSP. LIGHT MISO
⅓ CUP TAHINI (SESAME BUTTER)
1 CLOVE GARLIC, PEELED
1 TSP. LEMON ZEST
1 TSP. FRESH LEMON JUICE
1 TBSP. CHIVES

Place the sugar snap peas in a serving bowl and chill.

Place all remaining ingredients in the Single Serve Cup and pulse until smooth. Drizzle the sauce over the sugar snap peas and serve. Serves 4.

CAL 158, FAT 12G, SAT FAT 2G, CHOL 2MG, SODIUM 196MG,
CARBS 5G, PROTEIN 2G, FIBER 6G, CALCIUM 36MG, POTASSIUM 183MG

PARMESAN CAULIFLOWER CUPS

2 LBS. CAULIFLOWER FLORETS, STEAMED UNTIL SOFT AND COOLED
½ CUP LOW FAT SOUR CREAM
1 TSP. SALT
1 TSP. GROUND BLACK PEPPER
½ CUP PARMESAN CHEESE, GRATED, PLUS MORE FOR TOPPING

Preheat the oven to 375° degrees. Lightly coat 6 ramekins with cooking spray.

Place half each of the cauliflower, sour cream, salt, pepper and Parmesan cheese in the 40 oz. Processing Bowl. Pulse briefly. Repeat with the remaining half of each ingredient. Portion out the mixture into the ramekins. Top with additional Parmesan cheese. Bake for 15 minutes, or until heated through and the cheese has become golden. Serves 6.

CAL 176, FAT 7G, SAT FAT 4G, CHOL 18MG, SODIUM 881MG,
CARBS 20G, PROTEIN 12G, FIBER 7G, CALCIUM 162MG, POTASSIUM 887MG

SPRINGTIME PEA PUREE

10 OZ. PKG. FROZEN PEAS, COOKED, DRAINED
¼ CUP MINT LEAVES
¼ CUP LOW FAT SOUR CREAM
1 TSP. SALT

Place the peas in the 40 oz. Processing Bowl. Pulse until evenly mixed. Add the remaining ingredients and pulse until smooth. Serve immediately or chill until serving. Serves 4.

CAL 88, FAT 3G, SAT FAT 2G, CHOL 10MG, SODIUM 23MG,
CARBS 9G, PROTEIN 4G, FIBER 5G, CALCIUM 55MG, POTASSIUM 67MG

TENDER-CRISP ASPARAGUS WITH HOLLANDAISE SAUCE

3 LARGE EGG YOLKS
2 TBSP. LEMON JUICE, DIVIDED
1 TBSP. WATER
1 TSP. DIJON MUSTARD
¾ CUP BUTTER, MELTED
2 TSP. FLAT LEAF PARSLEY
¼ TSP. SALT
⅛ TSP. CAYENNE PEPPER
1 LB. ASPARAGUS SPEARS, STEAMED TENDER-CRISP

Place the egg yolks, 1 tbsp. lemon juice, water and mustard in the 40 oz. Processing Bowl. Pulse well to combine. Continue pulsing while pouring the melted butter in a very slow, steady stream through the pour spout, until the sauce has thickened. Add the parsley, salt, cayenne pepper and pulse for a few seconds. Add some of the remaining lemon juice to reach your desired consistency.

Drizzle the Hollandaise sauce over the steamed asparagus to serve. Serves 4. *(Cook's note: Store any remaining sauce in the refrigerator and use within 1 day.)*

CAL 246, FAT 25G, SAT FAT 15G, CHOL 166MG, SODIUM 151MG, CARBS 3G, PROTEIN 3G, FIBER 2G, CALCIUM 41MG, POTASSIUM 181MG

TOMATOES GREMOLATA

4 LARGE BEEFSTEAK TOMATOES, CORED, SEEDED AND CUT IN-HALF CROSSWISE
SALT AND PEPPER FOR SEASONING
5 SLICES STALE BREAD
3 GREEN ONIONS, ROUGHLY CUT
12 FRESH BASIL LEAVES
½ CUP FLAT LEAF PARSLEY LEAVES
2 CLOVES GARLIC, PEELED
1 TBSP. LEMON ZEST
EXTRA VIRGIN OLIVE OIL
¼ CUP GRUYERE CHEESE, GRATED

Preheat the oven to 400°F. Place the tomatoes in a 9 x 13-inch casserole dish and season with salt and pepper. Place the bread, onions, basil, parsley, garlic, and lemon zest in the 40 oz. Processing Bowl and pulse until a bread crumb mixture is formed. Divide among the tomato halves, filling each tomato half compactly.

Drizzle each tomato with a little olive oil. Bake for 15 minutes. Top with the cheese and bake for an additional few minutes until the cheese has melted. Serves 4.

CAL 80, FAT 3G, SAT FAT 1G, CHOL 8MG, SODIUM 106MG,
CARBS 11G, PROTEIN 4G, FIBER 2G, CALCIUM 86MG, POTASSIUM 308MG

FRESH PEAR GALETTE – P. 181
PÂTE SUCRÉE – P. 182
PÂTE BRISÉE – P. 183
FRUIT CROSTADA – P. 184
QUEENSLAND BANANA BREAD – P. 185
DARK CHOCOLATE & CHERRY COOKIES – P. 186
SWEET CARROT COOKIES – P. 187
CANDIED GINGER COOKIES – P. 188
SLICE & BAKE BUTTERY LEMON COOKIES – P. 189
FIG & ALMOND GRANOLA BARS – P. 190
ALMOND MACAROONS – P. 191

CHAPTER SEVEN :: BREADS & BAKERY GOODS

WALNUT & RAISIN CINNAMON ROLLS – P. 192
RAISIN MOLASSES MUFFINS – P. 193
BLUEBERRY LEMON MUFFINS – P. 194
HONEY CREPES – P. 195
WHOLE WHEAT PIZZA/FLATBREAD DOUGH – P. 196
ITALIAN BREADSTICKS – P. 197
SUMMER VEGETABLE FLATBREAD – P. 198
APPLE, PROSCUITTO & CARAMELIZED ONION FLATBREAD – P. 199
MARGHERITA FLATBREAD – P. 200
WARM TOMATO & MOZZARELLA TART – P. 201

APPLE, PROSCUITTO AND CARAMELIZED ONION FLATBREAD – P. 199

HONEY CREPES – P. 195

QUEENSLAND BANANA BREAD – P. 185

FRESH PEAR GALETTE – P. 181

FRESH PEAR GALETTE

1 RECIPE PÂTE SUCRÉE (SEE FOLLOWING RECIPE)
3 TBSP. APRICOT PRESERVES
2 LARGE RIPE PEARS, THINLY SLICED
1 EGG, BEATEN
2 TBSP. RAW SUGAR

Preheat the oven to 375°F.

Roll the pastry dough on a floured board to form a 14-inch round. Place the dough on a baking sheet. Brush the dough with the apricot preserves and fan the pear slices into a circle, leaving a 2-inch border. Fold the border up and around the pears, pressing gently. Brush the edge of the dough with egg and sprinkle with the raw sugar. Bake for 40 to 45 minutes until crust is golden and the pears are baked through. Let stand for 15 minutes before serving. Serves 4 to 6.

CAL 206, FAT 10G, SAT FAT 8G, CHOL 48MG, SODIUM 80MG,
CARBS 26G, PROTEIN 5G, FIBER 11G, CALCIUM 15MG, POTASSIUM 86MG

PÂTE SUCRÉE (SWEET PASTRY DOUGH)

1 CUP UNBLEACHED, ALL-PURPOSE FLOUR
1 TBSP. SUGAR
1 EGG
⅛ TSP. SALT
6 TBSP. COLD BUTTER, CUT INTO SMALL PIECES
¼ CUP ICE WATER

Position the Dough Blade in the 40 oz. Processing Bowl. Add the flour, sugar, egg, salt and butter and pulse just until combined. Add the ice water all at once and pulse again until the dough forms a rough ball. Remove and make a firm ball; flatten to a round disk shape. Chill until using. Makes 1 pastry crust.

CAL 148, FAT 17G, SAT FAT 6G, CHOL 25MG, SODIUM 71MG,
CARBS 13G, PROTEIN 3G, FIBER 0G, CALCIUM 8MG, POTASSIUM 28MG

PÂTE BRISÉE
(BASIC PASTRY DOUGH)

⅔ CUP VEGETABLE SHORTENING
1 TSP. SALT
⅓ CUP WATER, PLUS 1 TABLESPOON AS NEEDED
2 CUPS UNBLEACHED, ALL PURPOSE FLOUR

Position the Dough Blade in the 40 oz. Processing Bowl. Add the shortening, salt and one-third cup water and pulse briefly. Add the flour all at once and pulse again, scraping down the sides of the blender as needed. Add water as needed just until the dough begins to form.

Round the pastry into a ball and flatten to a round disk. Chill until ready to use. Makes 2 pastry crusts, serves 16. (Cook's note: this pastry is easy to roll and work with in pie and pastry recipes.)

CAL 133, FAT 9G, SAT FAT 3G, CHOL 18MG, SODIUM 15MG,
CARBS 12G, PROTEIN 2G, FIBER 0G, CALCIUM 2MG, POTASSIUM 17MG

FRUIT CROSTADA

¼ CUP SUGAR
2 CUPS FLOUR
½ TSP. KOSHER SALT
1 CUP COLD BUTTER, CUT INTO SMALL PIECES
¼ CUP ICE WATER
2 CUPS FRESH FRUIT, ROUGHLY CUT
3 TBSP. SUPERFINE SUGAR

Position the Dough Blade in the 40 oz. Processing Bowl and add the sugar. Pulse for 30 seconds. Add the flour and salt and pulse again. Add the butter and pulse until the mixture resembles small peas.

Pour the ice water through the pour-spout and pulse quickly, just until the dough starts to form a mixture. Spoon out onto foil and quickly press together to form a rough disk. Cover and chill for 1 hour or in the freezer for 15-20 minutes.

Preheat the oven to 450˚F. Heavily flour a large piece of plastic wrap and quickly add the dough. Cover with another floured piece of wrap and roll to an 11-inch circle. Remove the wrap pieces and place the dough on a cookie sheet. Toss the fruit gently with sugar and place in the center of the dough, leaving a 1½-inch border. Fold up and pleat around the outside edge to encase the fruit. Bake for 20-25 minutes, or until the dough is golden. Serves 6 to 8.

CAL 380, FAT 24G, SAT FAT 15G, CHOL 61MG, SODIUM 310MG,
CARBS 40G, PROTEIN 4G, FIBER 1G, CALCIUM 18MG, POTASSIUM 104MG

QUEENSLAND BANANA BREAD

¼ CUP BUTTER
1 EGG
¾ CUP SUGAR
2 BANANAS, PEELED AND CUT IN HALF
3 TBSP. WHOLE MILK
½ TSP. BAKING SODA
½ TSP. BAKING POWDER
2 CUPS UNBLEACHED, ALL-PURPOSE FLOUR
½ CUP MACADAMIA NUTS, CHOPPED

Preheat the oven to 350°F. Position the Dough Blade into the 40 oz. Processing Bowl. Add the butter, egg, sugar, bananas and milk to the Bowl and pulse until combined. Add the soda, powder, flour and macadamias and pulse again briefly. Scrape down the sides of the Bowl as needed.

Lightly coat a 9 x 5-inch loaf pan with cooking spray and spoon the bread into the pan. Bake for 30 to 40 minutes, or until a toothpick comes out clean in the middle. Cool before slicing. Makes 1 loaf; 10 servings.

CAL 266, FAT 11G, SAT FAT 4G, CHOL 31MG, SODIUM 49MG,
CARBS 51G, PROTEIN 4G, FIBER 2G, CALCIUM 14MG, POTASSIUM 144MG

DARK CHOCOLATE & CHERRY COOKIES

½ CUP BUTTER
3 EGG WHITES
1 TSP. VANILLA EXTRACT
1 CUP DARK BROWN SUGAR
1 TSP. GROUND CINNAMON
1 CUP WHOLE WHEAT PASTRY FLOUR
1 CUP OAT BRAN
1 TSP. BAKING SODA
¼ TSP. SALT
1 TBSP. GROUND FLAXSEEDS
1 CUP DARK SEMI-SWEET CHOCOLATE CHIPS
1 CUP DRIED SWEET CHERRIES, ROUGHLY CHOPPED (OR USE DRIED CRANBERRIES)

Preheat oven to 350°F. Place the Cookie Paddle in the 40 oz. Processing Bowl and add the butter, egg whites and vanilla. Pulse until creamy. Add the sugar, cinnamon, flour, oat bran, baking soda, salt, and flaxseeds and pulse until just combined. Transfer to a mixing bowl and add the chocolate chips and cherries by hand. Cover and chill for 10 minutes.

Drop the dough by tablespoons onto nonstick cookie sheets, leaving an inch between each cookie. Bake until golden, about 10 minutes. Makes 3 dozen.

CAL 200, FAT 6G, SAT FAT 3G, CHOL 7MG, SODIUM 137MG,
CARBS 38G, PROTEIN 4G, FIBER 3G, CALCIUM 38MG, POTASSIUM 82MG

SWEET CARROT COOKIES

1 CUP VEGETABLE SHORTENING
¾ CUP SUGAR
2 EGGS
1 CUP CARROTS, PEELED, GRATED
2 CUPS FLOUR
2 TSP. BAKING POWDER
½ TSP. SALT

Preheat the oven to 375°F.

Position the Cookie Paddle in the 40 oz. Processing Bowl and add all ingredients. Pulse just until combined. Do not over-mix. Drop the batter by teaspoons onto a cookie sheet that has been lightly coated with cooking spray. Bake for 8 to 10 minutes. Makes about 3 dozen cookies; 2 cookies per serving.

CAL 196, FAT 12G, SAT FAT 5G, CHOL 27MG, SODIUM 118MG, CARBS 20G, PROTEIN 7G, FIBER 1G, CALCIUM 45MG, POTASSIUM 42MG

CANDIED GINGER COOKIES

1¼ CUPS UNBLEACHED, ALL-PURPOSE FLOUR
1 CUP WHOLE WHEAT PASTRY FLOUR
2 TSP. GROUND GINGER
1 TSP. GROUND CINNAMON
½ TSP. GROUND CLOVES
¼ TSP. SALT
¾ CUP BUTTER
¾ CUP RAW, UNFILTERED HONEY
1 EGG
2 TBSP. BLACKSTRAP MOLASSES
2 TBSP. CANDIED GINGER, FINELY CHOPPED

Preheat the oven to 350°F.

Whisk the flours, ginger, cinnamon, cloves and salt until combined. Set aside. Place the Cookie Paddle in the 40 oz. Processing Bowl and pulse the butter, honey, egg and molasses until well-combined. Add the dry ingredients and the ginger and pulse just until mixed.

Chill dough for 10 minutes. Drop the dough by teaspoonsful on nonstick cookie sheets about 1 inch apart. Bake for 8 to 10 minutes and cool on wire racks before serving. Makes 3 dozen; 2 per serving.

CAL 132, FAT 8G, SAT FAT 4G, CHOL 12MG, SODIUM 172MG,
CARBS 29G, PROTEIN 5G, FIBER 1G, CALCIUM 22MG, POTASSIUM 67MG

SLICE & BAKE BUTTERY LEMON COOKIES

1 CUP BUTTER
½ CUP RAW SUGAR
⅛ TSP. SALT
1 LARGE EGG
1 TSP. LEMON EXTRACT
1 CUP WHOLE WHEAT PASTRY FLOUR
1½ CUPS UNBLEACHED ALL-PURPOSE FLOUR

Position the Cookie Paddle in the 40 oz. Processing Bowl and place the butter and sugar inside. Pulse until fluffy. Add the salt, egg and lemon extract and blend until smooth. Add the flours and pulse until just combined. Remove dough from the Bowl and roll into two logs. Wrap each log in plastic wrap and place in the refrigerator to chill for at least 1 hour.

Preheat the oven to 400°F. Remove dough from the plastic wrap and cut to form ¼-inch thick slices. Place onto nonstick cookie sheets and bake for 8 to 10 minutes until slightly golden brown. Cool on wire racks before serving. Makes about 3 dozen; 1 cookie per serving.

CAL 194, FAT 11G, SAT FAT 7G, CHOL 37MG, SODIUM 91MG,
CARBS 17G, PROTEIN 2G, FIBER 0G, CALCIUM 11MG, POTASSIUM 39MG

FIG & ALMOND GRANOLA BARS

1 CUP ROLLED OATS
½ CUP SHELLED, UNSALTED RAW SUNFLOWER SEEDS
½ CUP TOASTED WHEAT GERM
¼ CUP WHOLE WHEAT PASTRY FLOUR
½ CUP DRIED FIGS, ROUGHLY CHOPPED (OR USE ANY DRIED FRUIT)
½ CUP RAW ALMONDS
½ CUP NONFAT DRY MILK
1 TSP. GROUND CINNAMON
¼ CUP RAW, UNFILTERED HONEY
¼ CUP PURE MAPLE SYRUP
2 LARGE EGGS

Preheat oven to 350°F. Coat a 9 x 9-inch baking pan with cooking spray. Set aside.

Place the oats, sunflower seeds, wheat germ, flour, figs, almonds, dried milk, and cinnamon into the 40 oz. Processing Bowl and pulse 5 or 6 times. Add the honey, syrup, and eggs and pulse until combined. Place the dough into the baking pan and use a spatula to evenly spread. Bake for 20 minutes, until lightly browned. Allow to cool for 15 minutes before slicing into bars 1 x 3 inches. Makes about 27 bars; 2 bars per serving.

CAL 133, FAT 5G, SAT FAT 1G, CHOL 21MG, SODIUM 19MG,
CARBS 19G, PROTEIN 4G, FIBER 2G, CALCIUM 54MG, POTASSIUM 158MG

ALMOND MACAROONS

½ CUP ORANGE JUICE
2 CUPS BLANCHED ALMONDS, DIVIDED
2 CUPS SUGAR, DIVIDED
6 EGG WHITES, DIVIDED
4 TBSP. CAKE FLOUR, DIVIDED
¼ TSP. SALT, DIVIDED
⅔ CUP POWDERED SUGAR

Preheat oven to 300°F. Place the orange juice, 1 cup almonds and 1 cup sugar in the 40 oz. Processing Bowl. Pulse for 1 minute until very fine. Add the remaining almonds and pulse for another 30 seconds. Transfer one-half of the dough to a self-sealing plastic bag and chill.

Add half of the remaining ingredients to the dough in the Bowl and pulse until incorporated. Drop by teaspoons onto parchment-covered baking sheets. Let stand 30 minutes, then bake for 25 minutes. Repeat with the remaining almond paste and cookie ingredients. Cool completely before serving. Makes about 3 dozen cookies; 2 cookies per serving.

CAL 208, FAT 8G, SAT FAT 1G, CHOL 0MG, SODIUM 51MG,
CARBS 33G, PROTEIN 5G, FIBER 2G, CALCIUM 42MG, POTASSIUM 151MG

WALNUT & RAISIN CINNAMON ROLLS

1 PKG. ACTIVE "QUICK RISE" DRY YEAST
¼ CUP RAW SUGAR
½ TSP. SALT
¼ CUP WARM WATER (110-115°F)
¾ CUP WARM WHOLE MILK
¼ CUP BUTTER, MELTED
1 EGG
3¼ CUPS UNBLEACHED, ALL-PURPOSE FLOUR
1 CUP BROWN SUGAR
1 TBSP. GROUND CINNAMON
½ CUP BUTTER, SOFTENED
¼ CUP TOASTED WALNUTS, CHOPPED
¼ CUP RAISINS

Position the Dough Blade in the 40 oz. Processing Bowl. Add the yeast, sugar, salt, water, milk, butter and egg and pulse 2 to 3 times. Mix in the flour a quarter cup at a time, pulsing after each addition. Pulse off and on for 2 minutes, adding more flour if needed to form a soft dough. Place dough in a greased bowl, cover and let rise for 1 hour. Meanwhile, combine the brown sugar, cinnamon, and butter in a medium bowl.

Preheat the oven to 350°F. Roll the dough into a large rectangle and spread with the cinnamon mixture. Sprinkle with walnuts and raisins. Roll up the dough like a jelly roll. Pinch seam and ends. Cut into 12 rolls. Place in a greased 9 x 13-inch pan. Cover and let rise an additional 45 minutes. Bake for 25 minutes or until golden. Makes 12 rolls.

CAL 343, FAT 14G, SAT FAT 7G, CHOL 48MG, SODIUM 200MG,
CARBS 50G, PROTEIN 5G, FIBER 1G, CALCIUM 50MG, POTASSIUM 173MG

RAISIN MOLASSES MUFFINS

1 CUP WHOLE WHEAT FLOUR
1½ CUPS WHEAT BRAN
½ TSP. SALT
1 TSP. BAKING SODA
2 LARGE EGGS
1½ CUPS LOW FAT BUTTERMILK
3 TBSP. CANOLA OIL
1 TBSP. BLACKSTRAP MOLASSES
½ CUP DARK BROWN SUGAR
½ CUP RAISINS

Preheat oven to 400°F. Position the Dough Blade in the 40 oz. Processing Bowl. Add the flour, bran, salt and soda and pulse 1 or 2 times. Add the eggs, buttermilk, oil, molasses and sugar and pulse again just until combined. Add the raisins by hand and spoon into prepared muffin tins. Bake for 15-20 minutes. Makes 12 muffins.

CAL 180, FAT 8G, SAT FAT 5G, CHOL 36MG, SODIUM 144MG,
CARBS 27G, PROTEIN 2G, FIBER 1G, CALCIUM 47MG, POTASSIUM 119MG

BLUEBERRY LEMON MUFFINS

1 CUP WHOLE WHEAT FLOUR
1 ⅔ CUPS UNBLEACHED, ALL-PURPOSE FLOUR
1 TBSP. BAKING SODA
½ CUP RAW, UNFILTERED HONEY
2 EGGS
¾ CUP WHOLE MILK
⅔ CUP BUTTER, MELTED
1½ CUPS FRESH BLUEBERRIES
3 TSP. LEMON ZEST

Preheat oven to 400°F.

Position the Dough Blade in the 40 oz. Processing Bowl. Place the flours and soda in the Bowl and add the honey, eggs, milk and melted butter. Pulse just until combined. Fold in the blueberries and lemon zest with a spoon and pour into prepared muffin tins. Bake for 18-20 minutes. Makes 12 muffins.

CAL 263, FAT 12G, SAT FAT 7G, CHOL 57MG, SODIUM 196MG,
CARBS 36G, PROTEIN 5G, FIBER 1G, CALCIUM 3MG, POTASSIUM 87MG

HONEY CREPES

2 LARGE EGGS
¾ CUP WHOLE MILK
½ CUP WATER
1 CUP UNBLEACHED, ALL-PURPOSE FLOUR
3 TBSP. BUTTER, MELTED
1 TSP. VANILLA EXTRACT
1 TBSP. RAW, UNFILTERED HONEY
OIL AS NEEDED
HONEY FOR DRIZZLING
POWDERED SUGAR

Place the Dough Blade in the 40 oz. Processing Bowl. Add the eggs, milk, water, flour, butter, vanilla, and 1 tablespoon honey and pulse until smooth.

In a nonstick sauté pan, heat a little oil over medium-high heat. Pour a small amount of batter into the pan and swirl around evenly to form a thin circle. Cook for 30 seconds. Flip and cook for an additional 10 seconds. Remove and keep warm on a plate.

Continue with the remaining batter, stacking the crepes between layers of parchment paper. To serve, roll the crepes to form cigar shapes, place on a serving platter, and drizzle with honey. Sift with powdered sugar just before serving. Makes 4 servings; 2 crepes per serving.

CAL 272, FAT 12G, SAT FAT 6G, CHOL 118MG, SODIUM 145MG,
CARBS 29G, PROTEIN 10G, FIBER 1G, CALCIUM 126MG, POTASSIUM 218MG

WHOLE WHEAT PIZZA/ FLATBREAD DOUGH

¼ OZ. PKG. DRY ACTIVE YEAST
1 TSP. SALT
1 TBSP. SUGAR
⅔ CUP WARM WATER (110°-115°F)
¼ CUP EXTRA VIRGIN OLIVE OIL
1 CUP UNBLEACHED, ALL-PURPOSE FLOUR
1¼ CUPS WHOLE WHEAT FLOUR

Position the Dough Blade in the 40 oz. Processing Bowl. Place the yeast, salt, sugar and water inside and pulse briefly. Add the oil and flours, 1 cup at a time, pulsing 3 times between each addition. Pulse until a ball forms. Transfer dough to a lightly-oiled bowl and cover. Let rise for about an hour. Makes 1 pizza or flatbread.

(Cook's note: you can store this dough in the refrigerator, in a self-sealing plastic bag with a little olive oil, for up to one week.)

CAL 240, FAT 12G, SAT FAT 2G, CHOL 0MG, SODIUM 581MG,
CARBS 28G, PROTEIN 4G, FIBER 1G, CALCIUM 5MG, POTASSIUM 34MG

ITALIAN BREADSTICKS

1 WHOLE WHEAT PIZZA DOUGH (SEE PRECEDING RECIPE)
2 TBSP. EXTRA VIRGIN OLIVE OIL
1 TSP. DRIED OREGANO
1 TSP. DRIED ROSEMARY
¼ CUP PARMESAN CHEESE, GRATED

Preheat the oven to 375°F.

Roll the dough into a 6 x 8-inch rectangle. Cut the dough into ¾-inch strips. Twist each strip and place on a greased baking sheet. Cover and let rise in a warm place for 1 hour. Brush with oil and sprinkle with the oregano, rosemary, and cheese. Bake for 12 to 15 minutes until golden brown. Makes 10 to 12 breadsticks.

CAL 284, FAT 16G, SAT FAT 3G, CHOL 0MG, SODIUM 623MG,
CARBS 28G, PROTEIN 4G, FIBER 1G, CALCIUM 40MG, POTASSIUM 38MG

SUMMER VEGETABLE FLATBREAD

1 SMALL ZUCCHINI, SLICED INTO ¼-INCH THICK ROUNDS
1 SMALL RED PEPPER, SLICED INTO ¼-INCH WIDE STRIPS
1 SMALL EGGPLANT, SLICED INTO ¼-INCH THICK ROUNDS
2 TBSP. EXTRA VIRGIN OLIVE OIL
SALT AND PEPPER TO TASTE
1 WHOLE WHEAT PIZZA DOUGH (SEE P. 196)
½ CUP FONTINA CHEESE, SHREDDED
¼ CUP PARMESAN CHEESE, GRATED
CORNMEAL FOR DUSTING

Preheat the broiler to High. In a large mixing bowl, combine the zucchini, pepper and eggplant and toss with the olive oil, salt and pepper. Place the vegetables in a single layer on a baking sheet and broil for 8 minutes, turning once halfway through.

Heat the oven to 450°F. Sprinkle a 10 x 15-inch baking sheet with cornmeal and roll out or press the dough by hand on the sheet. It should be very thin. Top with the broiled vegetables and scatter the cheeses over the top. Bake for 10 to 15 minutes, until cheeses are melted and crust is golden brown. (For a crisper crust, use a pizza stone for baking.) Serves 4 to 6.

CAL 412, FAT 25G, SAT FAT 7G, CHOL 20MG, SODIUM 772MG,
CARBS 38G, PROTEIN 10G, FIBER 6G, CALCIUM 152MG, POTASSIUM 442MG

APPLE, PROSCUITTO, & CARAMELIZED ONION FLATBREAD

1 WHOLE WHEAT PIZZA DOUGH (SEE P. 196)
½ CUP CRÈME FRAICHE
1 LARGE YELLOW ONION, THINLY SLICED AND CARAMELIZED IN A SAUTÉ PAN
4 SLICES PROSCUITTO, BROWNED AND CRUMBLED (OR USE BACON)
½ SMALL FUJI APPLE, THINLY SLICED
¼ CUP ROMANO CHEESE, GRATED
2 TBSP. FLAT-LEAF PARSLEY
CORNMEAL FOR DUSTING

Preheat the oven to 450°F.

Sprinkle a 10 x 15-inch baking sheet with cornmeal and roll out or press the dough by hand on the sheet. It should be very thin. Spread a thin layer of crème fraiche over the flatbread and layer with the onions, proscuitto, apple slices, and cheese. Scatter the parsley over all and bake for 10 to 15 minutes, until the cheese has melted and the crust is golden brown. (For a crisper crust, use a pizza stone for baking.) Serves 4 to 6.

CAL 383, FAT 25G, SAT FAT 12G, CHOL 57MG, SODIUM 615MG,
CARBS 25G, PROTEIN 13G, FIBER 2G, CALCIUM 250MG, POTASSIUM 98MG

MARGHERITA FLATBREAD

1 WHOLE WHEAT PIZZA DOUGH (SEE P. 196)
3 TBSP. TOMATO SAUCE
1 MEDIUM BEEFSTEAK TOMATO, THINLY SLICED
4 OZ. FRESH MOZZARELLA BALL, THINLY SLICED
10 FRESH BASIL LEAVES, DIVIDED
EXTRA VIRGIN OLIVE OIL
CORNMEAL FOR DUSTING

Preheat the oven to 450°F.

Sprinkle a 10 x 15-inch baking sheet with cornmeal and roll out or press the dough by hand on the sheet. It should be very thin. Brush with the tomato sauce. Top with the tomato slices, mozzarella slices, and half of the basil leaves. Bake for 10 to 15 minutes, until the cheese has melted and the crust is golden brown. Top with the remaining basil leaves and a drizzle of olive oil before serving. Serves 4.

CAL 348, FAT 22G, SAT FAT 5G, CHOL 10MG, SODIUM 621MG,
CARBS 30G, PROTEIN 8G, FIBER 2G, CALCIUM 109MG, POTASSIUM 132MG

WARM TOMATO & MOZZARELLA TART

1 CUP UNBLEACHED ALL-PURPOSE FLOUR
¼ TSP. SALT
6 TBSP. COLD BUTTER, CUT IN SMALL PIECES
¼ CUP COLD WATER
½ CUP MOZZARELLA CHEESE, SHREDDED
1 SMALL ONION, PEELED AND SLICED
2 ROMA TOMATOES, SLICED
COARSE SEA SALT
GROUND BLACK PEPPER
2 TBSP. FRESH BASIL

Preheat the oven to 400°F.

Position the Dough Blade in the 40 oz. Processing Bowl and add the flour, salt and butter. Pulse until crumbly. Add the water and pulse again until the pastry forms into a rough ball. Form into a flattened disk.

Roll the pastry dough to a 14-inch circle and fit into a 10-inch tart pan (or use a pie pan), trimming the edges.

Layer the cheese, onion and tomatoes over the pastry and sprinkle with the salt and pepper. Scatter the basil over all. Bake for 30 to 35 minutes. Cut into wedges and serve while warm. Serves 4 to 6.

CAL 237, FAT 15G, SAT FAT 9G, CHOL 43MG, SODIUM 420MG,
CARBS 19G, PROTEIN 7G, FIBER 1G, CALCIUM 161MG, POTASSIUM 116MG

ITALIAN TIRAMISU PARFAITS – P. 207
SILKY LEMON CREAM WITH BLUEBERRIES – P. 208
ALMOND SHORTCRUST – P. 209
FRESH FRUIT & LEMON CREAM TART – P. 210
STRAWBERRY BASIL ICE CREAM – P. 211
CREAMY DREAMY CHEESECAKE – P. 212
ALMOND SOUR CREAM CHEESECAKE – P. 213
BERRY BERRY CRISP – P. 214

CHAPTER EIGHT :: DELECTABLE DESSERTS

PUMPKIN PIE – P. 215
MANGO PEACH FROZEN YOGURT – P. 216
FRUIT N' CREAM ICE CREAM – P. 217
FRESH MANGO FOOL – P. 218
CANTALOUPE MINT GRANITA – P. 219
PINEAPPLE GINGER COCONUT SORBET – P. 220
TART BLUEBERRY SORBET – P. 221
GREEN TEA GRANITA – P. 222

FRESH MANGO FOOL – P. 218

CREAMY DREAMY CHEESECAKE – P. 212

ITALIAN TIRAMISU PARFAITS – P. 207

BERRY BERRY CRISP – P. 214

ITALIAN TIRAMISU PARFAITS

8 OZ. MASCARPONE CHEESE
2 TBSP. SUGAR
2 TBSP. BRANDY
1 PKG. LADYFINGERS
1½ CUPS STRONG COFFEE
1 CUP WHIPPED CREAM
TOASTED ALMONDS
SHAVED CHOCOLATE

Position the Dough Blade in the 40 oz. Processing Bowl. Place the cheese, sugar and brandy in the Bowl and pulse until smooth.

To assemble 4 parfaits, spoon a small amount of the cheese mixture in each of 4 wide glasses. Dip 2 ladyfingers into the coffee and place on top of the cheese. Repeat with another layer of cheese to each parfait and repeat with the ladyfingers. Repeat the layers until the ingredients are used. Add a dollop of whipped cream to each parfait. Finish each with toasted almonds and shaved chocolate. Serve at once. Serves 4.

CAL 249, FAT 19G, SAT FAT 11G, CHOL 57MG, SODIUM 26MG,
CARBS 12G, PROTEIN 3G, FIBER 0G, CALCIUM 10MG, POTASSIUM 11MG

SILKY LEMON CREAM WITH BLUEBERRIES

4 OZ. LOW FAT CREAM CHEESE
¾ CUP PLAIN GREEK YOGURT
½ TSP. LEMON EXTRACT
2 TBSP. RAW, UNFILTERED HONEY
2 CUPS FRESH BLUEBERRIES, RINSED

Place the cream cheese, yogurt, lemon extract and honey in the 40 oz. Processing Bowl. Pulse until whipped and smooth.

Layer the lemon cream and blueberries in dessert dishes or wineglasses. Chill or serve at once. Serves 4.

CAL 164, FAT 7G, SAT FAT 4G, CHOL 18MG, SODIUM 106MG,
CARBS 23G, PROTEIN 9G, FIBER 2G, CALCIUM 89MG, POTASSIUM 113MG

ALMOND SHORTCRUST

2 TBSP. BLANCHED, WHOLE ALMONDS
1¾ CUPS ALL-PURPOSE FLOUR
¼ CUP + 1 TBSP. POWDERED SUGAR
6 TBSP. BUTTER, SOFTENED
PINCH KOSHER SALT
1 VANILLA BEAN, SEEDED, POD DISCARDED
2 EGG YOLKS

Place the almonds in the 40 oz. Processing Bowl. Process the nuts until finely ground. Add the remaining ingredients and pulse until the dough forms a ball. Cover and chill for 30 minutes.

Preheat the oven to 350°F. To prepare a tart pastry, roll out the dough between two sheets of plastic wrap and fit into a tart pan. Place the pan on a cookie sheet and bake for 20 minutes. Fill as your recipe directs. Makes 1 large or 2 medium tart shells.

CAL 186, FAT 10G, SAT FAT 5G, CHOL 60MG, SODIUM 67MG, CARBS 22G, PROTEIN 4G, FIBER 1G, CALCIUM 17MG, POTASSIUM 50MG

FRESH FRUIT & LEMON CREAM TART

16 OZ. LOW FAT CREAM CHEESE (OR USE NEUCHATEL CHEESE), SOFTENED
⅓ CUP SUGAR
1 LEMON, JUICED
1 RECIPE ALMOND SHORTCRUST DOUGH, BAKED AND COOLED (SEE P. 209)
2½ PINTS FRESH FRUIT, SUCH AS BERRIES, KIWI OR STONE FRUIT (SLICED)
1 CUP CURRANT JELLY, MELTED (OR USE OTHER FRUIT JELLY)

Position the Dough Paddle in the 40 oz. Processing Bowl and add the cream cheese, sugar and lemon juice. Pulse until smooth.

Spoon the cream cheese mixture evenly onto the cooled pastry and smooth the top with a knife. Arrange the fruit in concentric circles over the cheese mixture and brush with the melted jelly. Chill to set. Serves 10.

CAL 406, FAT 18G, SAT FAT 10G, CHOL 85MG, SODIUM 210MG,
CARBS 55G, PROTEIN 10G, FIBER 2G, CALCIUM 73MG, POTASSIUM 305MG

STRAWBERRY BASIL ICE CREAM

2 CUPS STRAWBERRIES, STEMMED AND HULLED
1 CUP SUGAR
15 FRESH BASIL LEAVES
2 CUPS WHOLE MILK
2 CUPS LIGHT CREAM
2 TSP. VANILLA EXTRACT

Place the strawberries, sugar and basil in the 40 oz. Processing Bowl. Pulse until the strawberry mixture is smooth. Spoon into a large bowl, add the remaining ingredients and stir to combine.

Pour the ice cream mixture into the freezer bowl or tub of your ice cream maker and proceed as directed. Makes 1 quart.

CAL 225, FAT 9G, SAT FAT 6G, CHOL 29MG, SODIUM 50MG,
CARBS 34G, PROTEIN 4G, FIBER 1G, CALCIUM 140MG, POTASSIUM 223MG

CREAMY DREAMY CHEESECAKE

10 GRAHAM CRACKERS
¼ CUP SUGAR
¼ CUP BUTTER
2-8 OZ. PKGS. LOW FAT CREAM CHEESE, SOFTENED
1 CUP MASCARPONE CHEESE
1 TBSP. FRESH LEMON JUICE
1 CUP WHIPPED CREAM
¼ CUP SUGAR

Prepare crust by placing the crackers, sugar and butter in the 40 oz. Processing Bowl. Pulse until fine crumbs form. Press into a springform pan and refrigerate.

Meanwhile, mix together the remaining ingredients in the 40 oz. Processing Bowl until smooth. Pour into the crust and chill for at least 1 hour before serving. Serves 12.

CAL 357, FAT 29G, SAT FAT 18G, CHOL 80MG, SODIUM 236MG,
CARBS 20G, PROTEIN 8G, FIBER 0G, CALCIUM 64MG, POTASSIUM 100MG

ALMOND SOUR CREAM CHEESECAKE

8 OZ. LOW FAT CREAM CHEESE, SOFTENED
½ CUP SUGAR
1 TSP. ALMOND EXTRACT
½ TSP. VANILLA EXTRACT
2 LARGE EGGS
1 CUP SOUR CREAM
8-INCH PREPARED GRAHAM CRACKER CRUST
¼ CUP SLICED ALMONDS, TOASTED

Preheat the oven to 325°F. Position the Dough Blade in the 40 oz. Processing Bowl and add the cream cheese, sugar, almond extract, vanilla extract, eggs and sour cream. Pulse until smooth. Pour the filling into the prepared crust and smooth the top.

Bake for 25 minutes or until set in the center. Remove from the oven and let cool. Top with the toasted almonds. Serves 10.

CAL 311, FAT 16G, SAT FAT 6G, CHOL 67MG, SODIUM 270MG,
CARBS 35G, PROTEIN 7G, FIBER 4G, CALCIUM 108MG, POTASSIUM 108MG

BERRY BERRY CRISP

FILLING:

4 CUPS MIXED STRAWBERRIES, BLACKBERRIES AND RASPBERRIES
½ CUP SUGAR
2 TBSP. MINUTE OR INSTANT TAPIOCA
1 TSP. FRESH LIME JUICE

TOPPING:

⅓ CUP WALNUTS, CHOPPED
¼ CUP BUTTER, CUT IN SMALL PIECES
½ CUP UNBLEACHED, ALL PURPOSE FLOUR
⅓ CUP SUGAR
¼ TSP. BAKING POWDER
PINCH SALT

Preheat the oven to 375°F and lightly coat a 9 x 9-inch baking pan with cooking spray. Set aside.

Place the mixed berries in a bowl and add the sugar, tapioca and lime juice. Toss to coat evenly. Spoon into the prepared pan.

Place the walnuts, butter, flour, sugar, baking powder and salt in the 40 oz. Processing Bowl. Pulse until the walnuts are chopped and the mixture is crumbly. Scatter the topping over the fruit and bake for 35 to 40 minutes until bubbly. Serves 8 to 10.

CAL 176, FAT 7G, SAT FAT 3G, CHOL 12MG, SODIUM 58MG,
CARBS 28G, PROTEIN 1G, FIBER 2G, CALCIUM 15MG, POTASSIUM 110MG

PUMPKIN PIE

1 MEDIUM SUGAR PUMPKIN, CUT IN HALF; STEM, SEEDS AND STRINGY PULP REMOVED
12 OZ. CAN EVAPORATED MILK
1 CUP DARK BROWN SUGAR
½ TSP. SALT
3 EGGS
2 TSP. GROUND CINNAMON
1 TSP. GROUND GINGER
¼ TSP. GROUND NUTMEG
¼ TSP. GROUND CLOVES
¼ TSP. GROUND CARDAMOM
9-INCH PÂTE BRISÉE (SEE P. 183)

Preheat the oven to 350°F.

Place the sugar pumpkin halves on a lined baking sheet and bake, cut-side down, for 1 to 1½ hours, until flesh is very soft. Remove from the oven and let cool. Scrape out the pumpkin flesh.

Place 2 cups of the pumpkin flesh in the 40 oz. Processing Bowl and pulse until smooth. Spoon into a large bowl and add the remaining ingredients except the pie shell. Mix to combine and pour into the prepared pie crust. Bake for 1 hour until lightly browned and the middle is firm. Serves 8.

CAL 351, FAT 14G, SAT FAT 6G, CHOL 93MG, SODIUM 247MG, CARBS 49G, PROTEIN 8G, FIBER 2G, CALCIUM 181MG, POTASSIUM 279MG

MANGO PEACH FROZEN YOGURT

½ CUP FROZEN MANGO CHUNKS

½ CUP FROZEN PEACHES

2 CUPS LOW FAT VANILLA YOGURT

Place the mango, peaches and yogurt in the 40 oz. Processing Bowl. Pulse until smooth. Serve right away. Serves 4.

CAL 102, FAT 2G, SAT FAT 2G, CHOL 2MG, SODIUM 85MG,
CARBS 5G, PROTEIN 12G, FIBER 1G, CALCIUM 103MG, POTASSIUM 213MG

FRUIT N' CREAM ICE CREAM

2 CUPS FROZEN FRUIT (MIXED BERRIES, STRAWBERRIES, PEACHES ETC.)

½ CUP HEAVY CREAM (OR USE MILK OR LOW FAT MILK)

2-4 TBSP. SUGAR

1 TSP. VANILLA EXTRACT

Place all ingredients in the 40 oz. Processing Bowl. Pulse until smooth. Serves 6.

CAL 161, FAT 11G, SAT FAT 7G, CHOL 41MG, SODIUM 12MG,
CARBS 15G, PROTEIN 0G, FIBER 1G, CALCIUM 31MG, POTASSIUM 133MG

FRESH MANGO FOOL

2 MANGOS, PEELED AND SEEDED
½ CUP SUGAR SYRUP
1 CUP WHIPPED CREAM

Place the mango flesh and sugar syrup in the 40 oz. Processing Bowl and pulse until smooth. Spoon the mango mixture into a medium bowl and fold in the whipped cream. Serve right away in stemmed glasses. Serves 4.

CAL 182, FAT 11G, SAT FAT 7G, CHOL 21MG, SODIUM 14MG, CARBS 29G, PROTEIN 2G, FIBER 2G, CALCIUM 30MG, POTASSIUM 184MG

CANTALOUPE MINT GRANITA

1 RIPE CANTALOUPE, SEEDED, RIND REMOVED, AND CUT INTO CHUNKS
1 TBSP. FRESH LEMON JUICE
2 TBSP. WATER
2 TBSP. RAW, UNFILTERED HONEY
1 TBSP. FRESH MINT LEAVES

Place all of the ingredients in the 40 oz. Processing Bowl and pulse until completely smooth. Pour into a non-reactive dish or ice cube trays and freeze for 3 to 4 hours, until completely solid.

Just before serving, place the frozen cubes in the 40 oz. Processing Bowl and pulse again until smooth. Serve immediately. Serves 4.

CAL 79, FAT 0G, SAT FAT 0G, CHOL 0MG, SODIUM 85MG,
CARBS 22G, PROTEIN 2G, FIBER 1G, CALCIUM 18MG, POTASSIUM 371MG

PINEAPPLE GINGER COCONUT SORBET

1 SMALL RIPE PINEAPPLE, PEELED, CORED, ROUGHLY CUT
1 TBSP. FRESH LIME JUICE
½ CUP LIGHT COCONUT MILK
½ CUP SUPERFINE SUGAR
1 TSP. FRESH GINGER, CHOPPED

Place the pineapple in the 40 oz. Processing Bowl and pulse until smooth. Pour into a medium bowl. Place all of the remaining ingredients in the Bowl. Blend until completely smooth and add to the pineapple. Stir lightly to mix.

Pour the sorbet mixture into the freezer bowl or tub of your ice cream maker and proceed as directed. Makes about 1 quart.

CAL 114, FAT 1G, SAT FAT 1G, CHOL 0MG, SODIUM 4MG,
CARBS 28G, PROTEIN 1G, FIBER 2G, CALCIUM 15MG, POTASSIUM 124MG

TART BLUEBERRY SORBET

5 CUPS FROZEN BLUEBERRIES
½ CUP RAW, UNFILTERED HONEY
1 TSP. LEMON ZEST
1 TBSP. LEMON JUICE

Working in batches if needed, pulse the blueberries in the 40 oz. Processing Bowl until smooth. Place the blueberries in a large mixing bowl and add the honey, zest and juice. Mix well and place in your ice cream maker. Proceed as directed. Makes about 1 quart.

CAL 86, FAT 0G, SAT FAT 0G, CHOL 0MG, SODIUM 1MG,
CARBS 28G, PROTEIN 0G, FIBER 1G, CALCIUM 4MG, POTASSIUM 40MG

GREEN TEA GRANITA

3 CUPS WATER
3 GREEN TEA BAGS
¼ CUP RAW, UNFILTERED HONEY
1 TBSP. FRESH LEMON JUICE
FRESH MINT FOR GARNISH

Bring the water to a boil in a saucepan. Add the green tea and honey. Let steep for 15 minutes. Remove tea bags. Let cool and add the lemon juice. Mix to combine. Pour into ice cube trays. Let freeze for at least 3 hours, or until solid.

Place the frozen tea ice cubes in the 40 oz. Processing Bowl and pulse for 30 seconds. Garnish with mint leaves and serve immediately. Serves 4.

CAL 129, FAT 0G, SAT FAT 0G, CHOL 0MG, SODIUM 1MG,
CARBS 35G, PROTEIN 0G, FIBER 0G, CALCIUM 3MG, POTASSIUM 22MG

SEASONAL FRUIT & VEGETABLE GUIDE

	SPRING	SUMMER	FALL	WINTER
	MID MAR TO MID JUN	**MID JUN TO MID SEP**	**MID SEP TO MID DEC**	**MID DEC TO MID MAR**
FRUITS	Blueberries Strawberries	Blackberries Cantaloupe Cherries Grapes Honeydew Papayas Plums Peaches Watermelon Mangos Raspberries	Apples Pears Cranberries	Bananas Grapefruit Kiwis Oranges Pineapple
VEGETABLES	Asparagus Avocados Basil Beans Beets Broccoli Cabbage Chinese Cabbage Cucumbers Radish Iceberg Lettuce Okra Peas Chile Peppers Sweet Peppers Rhubarb Shallots Spinach Summer Squash Turnips	Basil Beans Beets Corn Cucumbers Dates Figs Okra Chile Peppers Sweet Peppers Summer Squash Tomatoes	Broccoli Brussels Sprouts Cabbage Chinese Cabbage Cauliflower Celery Root Chicory Cucumbers Dates Fennel Greens Leaf Lettuce Mushrooms Nuts Okra Chile Peppers Sweet Peppers Shallots Spinach Winter Squash Star Fruit Sweet Potatoes	Avocados Broccoli Brussels Sprouts Cabbage Chinese Cabbage Cauliflower Celery Root Chicory Fennel Greens Wild Mushrooms Spinach Sweet Potatoes

EQUIVALENTS CHART

WEIGHT MEASURES

USA/UK	METRIC
1 oz.	30 g.
2 oz.	60 g.
3 oz.	90 g.
4 oz. (1/4 lb.)	125 g.
5 oz. (1/3 lb.)	155 g.
6 oz.	185 g.
7 oz.	220 g.
8 oz. (1/2 lb.)	250 g.
10 oz.	315 g.
12 oz. (3/4 lb.)	375 g.
14 oz.	440 g
16 oz. (1 lb.)	500 g.
1½ lb.	750 g.
2 lb.	1 kg.
3 lb.	1½ kg.

LENGTH MEASURES

1/8 in.	3 mm.
1/4 in.	6 mm.
1/2 in.	12 mm.
1 in.	2.5 cm.

LIQUID MEASURES

USA	METRIC	UK
2 tbsp.	30 ml.	1 fl. oz.
1/4 cup	60 ml.	2 fl. oz.
1/3 cup	80 ml.	3 fl. oz.
1/2 cup	125 ml.	4 fl. oz.
2/3 cup	160 ml.	5 fl. oz.
3/4 cup	180 ml.	6 fl. oz.
1 cup	250 ml.	8 fl. oz.
1½ cups	375 ml.	12 fl. oz.
2 cups	500 ml.	16 fl. oz.

ABBREVIATIONS

USA/UK	METRIC
oz = ounce	g = gram
lb = pound	kg = kilogram
in = inch	mm = millimeter
ft = foot	cm = centimeter
tbsp = tablespoon	ml = milliliter
fl oz = fluid ounce	l = liter
qt = quart	